SERGEI O. PROKOFIEFF, born in Moscow in 1954, studied painting and art history at the Moscow School of Art. He encountered anthroposophy in his youth, and soon made the decision to devote his life to it. He has been active as an author and lecturer since 1982, and in 1991 he co-founded the Anthroposophical Society in Russia. In Easter 2001 he became a member of the Executive Council of the General Anthroposophical Society in Dornach. He is the author of many books, 25 of which have now been published in an English translation.

D1570264

By the same author:

Anthroposophy and The Philosophy of Freedom
The Cycle of the Seasons and the Seven Liberal Arts
The Cycle of the Year as a Path of Initiation
The East in the Light of the West, Parts One to Three
The Encounter with Evil and its Overcoming through Spiritual Science
The Esoteric Significance of Spiritual Work in Anthroposophical Groups
Eternal Individuality, Towards a Karmic Biography of Novalis
The Foundation Stone Meditation
The Guardian of the Threshold and The Philosophy of Freedom
The Heavenly Sophia and the Living Being Anthroposophia
May Human Beings Hear it!
The Mystery of John the Baptist and John the Evangelist
The Mystery of the Resurrection in the Light of Anthroposophy
The Occult Significance of Forgiveness
Prophecy of the Russian Epic
Relating to Rudolf Steiner
Rudolf Steiner and the Founding of the New Mysteries
Rudolf Steiner's Research into Karma and the Mission of the Anthroposophical Society
The Spiritual Origins of Eastern Europe and the Future Mysteries of the Holy Grail
The Twelve Holy Nights and the Spiritual Hierarchies
What is Anthroposophy?
The Whitsun Impulse

The Case of Valentin Tomberg
Valentin Tomberg, Rudolf Steiner and Anthroposophy

The Appearance of Christ in the Etheric
Spiritual-Scientific Aspects of the Second Coming

SERGEI O. PROKOFIEFF

TEMPLE LODGE

Translated from German by Simon Blaxland-de Lange

Temple Lodge Publishing
Hillside House, The Square
Forest Row, RH18 5ES

www.templelodge.com

Published by Temple Lodge 2012

Originally published in German under the title *Das Erscheinen des Christus im Ätherischen: Geisteswissenschaftliche Aspekte der ätherischen Wiederkunft* by Verlag am Goetheanum, Dornach, in 2010

A catalogue record for this book is available from the British Library

ISBN 978 1 906999 32 2

Cover by Andrew Morgan Design
Typeset by DP Photosetting, Neath, West Glamorgan
Printed and bound by Berforts, Herts.

Dedicated to the memory of Rudolf Steiner's first pronouncement about Christ in the etheric realm one hundred years ago

Contents

Introduction: A Brief Historical Survey   1

1. The Cosmic Dimension of Christ's Second Coming in the Etheric   3

2. The Appearance of Christ in the Etheric and the Being Anthroposophia   16

3. The Destiny of the Ego in the Age of the Etheric Christ   31

4. Memory and Conscience in the Light of the Second Coming   43

5. The Etheric Christ and the Michael Spirit Who Serves Him   52

6. The Second Coming and the Occult Powers that Oppose It   64
    Extract from Dostoyevsky's novel *Crime and Punishment*, Raskoinikov's vision   86

7. The Supersensible Mystery of Golgotha and Rudolf Steiner's Initiation   88

Conclusion: The Second Coming and the Tasks of the Anthroposophical Society   108

Appendix: The Relationship to Christ Today   113

Notes   136

Bibliography   158

Introduction: A Brief Historical Survey

'And as in former times the light of
the Spirit will shine brightly and
radiantly into the darkness: the Christ
will appear again on Earth, albeit in a
different form from before. We are
entrusted with the task of receiving
Him and serving Him.'

Rudolf Steiner [1]

It was in northern Europe, in Stockholm, that on 12 January 1910 Rudolf
Steiner began to speak about the appearance of the etheric Christ. A
number of lectures on this theme followed in anthroposophical branches
in central Europe and then, again in the north, there was a public lecture
in Kristiania (Oslo) on 13 June 1910. In the August of the same year these
tidings were expressed in artistic form in the first mystery play, *The Portal
of Initiation*, which bears the subtitle 'A Rosicrucian Mystery' (GA 14).
And in 1911 they were made fully public in the book *The Spiritual
Guidance of Man and Humanity* (GA 15).

Subsequently, in 1913, Rudolf Steiner spoke for the first time about
the supersensible Mystery of Golgotha as the spiritual foundation and
supersensible source of the etheric manifestation of Christ in the cultic
section of his esoteric school (see GA 265, 8 February 1913); and then on
2 May in the same year he spoke on this theme in a lecture for members in
London (see GA 152).

At the end of the year (in the lecture of 30 December) Rudolf Steiner
spoke for the first time about the three cosmic preparatory stages of the
Mystery of Golgotha (see GA 149). And at approximately the same time
he made his sketch for the central motif of the northern rose—or, to be
more precise, peach-blossom—window for the First Goetheanum, where
man's encounter with the etheric Christ was portrayed artistically for the
first time. [2]

The earliest, as yet only tentative indication of the imminent appearance of Christ in supersensible form was given in the esoteric lesson of 5
December 1907 in Munich. [3] Rudolf Steiner subsequently said that
Christ's approach in the etheric body was already perceptible for an
initiate from 1909 onwards on the astral plane, whereas it would become
accessible to humanity as a whole as a supersensible experience only from
the 1930s onwards (see GA 175, 6 February 1917).

After his first proclamation of this event of the supersensible world, which he described as the most important in our time and for the next 3000 years, Rudolf Steiner continued to speak about it until the end of his public lecturing activity. His last words on this theme were spoken in September 1924 in Dornach, in the cycle on the Book of Revelation for the priests of the Christian Community (GA 346). Thus this theme runs like a red thread through the whole development of anthroposophy, of which Rudolf Steiner said on several occasions that one of its most important tasks was to prepare mankind for this great spiritual event.

Thus in the 14 years between 1910 and 1924 Rudolf Steiner bore witness to this most important spiritual event of our time and the immediate future on all the levels accessible to him and in all manner of forms—oral, written and artistic. Summarizing all of this, an overview can now be given of all the realms where Rudolf Steiner has given indications concerning the Second Coming:

> lectures for members of the Theosophical (later the Anthroposophical) Society;
> lessons of the Esoteric School;
> lessons of instruction given in the cultic section of the Esoteric School;
> public lectures;
> the book *The Spiritual Guidance of Man and Humanity* (GA 15);
> the first mystery play, *The Portal of Initiation* (in GA 14);
> the northern rose-coloured window in the First (and Second) Goetheanum.

A systematic survey of all that Rudolf Steiner imparted about the Second Coming has not yet been made. However, it is quite certain today, more than 85 years after Rudolf Steiner's death, that the vast extent of the work and the great variety of the aspects and ideas regarding this theme that resulted from his endeavours enable him to be regarded as the greatest witness and servant of the etheric Christ.

The following observations are dedicated above all to the first proclamation of the Second Coming a century ago, and their intention is to portray certain aspects of this event on the basis of Rudolf Steiner's spiritual research.

1. The Cosmic Dimension of Christ's Second Coming in the Etheric

After his first statements about Christ's Second Coming in Stockholm on 12 January 1910 Rudolf Steiner referred the following year to the fact that this event forms the starting point of a sequence of ever higher revelations of Christ, of which two further ones were then described. (See GA 130, 17 September 1911.) Thus Christ's present manifestation in the etheric body on the astral plane, which will last for approximately three thousand years, will be followed by His next higher revelation in the astral body on the plane of Lower Devachan and then, in the far future, His appearance as the world Ego in Higher Devachan. In this way, mankind will be led step by step ever higher into the spiritual world. 'Thus we see how the Christ, once He has descended to the Earth, begins from the condition of a physical, earthly human being and gradually evolves as an etheric, astral and ego-Christ in order, as an ego-Christ, to become the Spirit of the Earth who then rises to higher stages with all human beings' (GA 130, 21 September 1911).

Subsequently, and for the first time on 30 December 1913 (GA 149), Rudolf Steiner spoke of how the Mystery of Golgotha, which forms the central axis of the whole evolution of the Earth and humanity, was preceded by three supersensible deeds on the part of Christ. At the end of the Lemurian age and on two subsequent occasions, at the beginning and the end of the Atlantean epoch, Christ brought these deeds about from the Sun in order on these three occasions to rescue mankind, which since the Fall had been constantly subject to the assaults of the adversarial powers. The first event had to do with the harmonizing of the twelve senses in the physical body; the second with the healing of the seven life-processes in man's etheric body; and finally, the third cosmic deed of Christ led to the three fundamental forces of the human soul—thinking, feeling and will—being brought into the necessary equilibrium for a right development of the ego. One can also say that, with this third step, man's astral body was rescued.

A particular feature of these three cosmic deeds was that Christ did not carry them out alone but through the mediation of a being who had been preserved in the spiritual world from the effects of the Fall, through which mankind had to descend to the Earth. Rudolf Steiner also calls this being the 'sister soul of Adam' (GA 142, 1 January 1913). In the Bible story this event is referred to in the imagination of the two trees in Paradise. Adam tastes of the Tree of Knowledge and begins his laborious path in and through the earthly world. The other being, however, remains connected with the Tree of Life. It is held back in the spiritual world and becomes there the guardian or preserver of man's eternal image, in accordance with which he had been originally created by the Gods (see GA 114, 18 September 1909).

Rudolf Steiner also indicates precisely where the original dwelling-place of this sister soul of Adam is to be sought: it was 'resident . . . on the Sun' (GA 149, 30 December 1913). This is not in contradiction with the fact that in an earlier lecture he brings it into connection with the Sun Lodge on the Earth, led by the great Manu (see GA 114, 18 September 1909). The apparent contradiction is resolved if one bears in mind that the Sun Lodge is the representative of the cosmic Sun realm on the Earth and is constantly in direct connection with it. And if Rudolf Steiner later reports that this sister soul of Adam was active in various mysteries (see GA 142, 1 January 1913), this activity emanated from the Sun through the mediation of the central Sun Lodge on the Earth.

Because this sister soul of Adam belonged from the outset to the Sun sphere, it was also associated with that being who—in the circle of Archangels guiding humanity—belongs pre-eminently to the Sun. 'But this special being, who is known esoterically by the name of Michael, is elevated above his companions to the same degree as the Sun is elevated above the planets' (GA 152, 2 May 1913). And as the Sun Archangel, Michael is also responsible for everything that happens in this cosmic realm. Thus it is owing to him that the sister soul of Adam evaded Adam's fate and did not fall prey to the Fall.[1] That Michael has continued to accompany this being through the three heavenly deeds referred to is attested by Rudolf Steiner above all through the example of the third deed, where he particularly emphasizes Michael's participation: 'Mankind formed a conception of this in the image of St George or St Michael, the dragon-slayer. This is a direct imaginative expression of the third har-binger of the event of Golgotha.' (GA 152, 30 March 1914.)

For the first and only time this special being incarnated on Earth at the Turning Point of Time as the Jesus described in St Luke's Gospel. And as Jesus of Nazareth it was—once it had received the qualities from the Zarathustra individuality that were necessary for this (see GA 131, 12 October 1911)—then entrusted with the task of being for three years the bearer of the Christ on Earth. And although everything on Earth was inevitably very strange at first to the Christ Being who had come directly from the Sun, there was this *one* being who had already been entrusted to

Him by the spiritual world. In several apocryphal traditions describing the childhood of this Jesus, facts are communicated which testify to the fact that this was indeed a heavenly being untouched by the Fall.

In these cosmic events referred to, which Rudolf Steiner also calls 'preliminary stages' of the Mystery of Golgotha, Christ on three occasions 'ensouled' the human being connected with Him and serving Him out of the realm of the Sun, the planets and the Moon sphere, in order to bring about the threefold rescuing of earthly humanity that has been described. Of particular importance in this respect is the first deed of Christ through the being who was to become Jesus of Nazareth, because something altogether new came about in the spiritual world as a result. 'Through being imbued with the Christ he [the future Jesus of Nazareth] then took on etheric human form. With this, something new entered the cosmos which now rays out upon both Earth and man, upon the physical earthly human form into which there streamed the force of the etheric, super-earthly Christ Being, thus making it possible for it to be protected from that force of destruction which would have had to enter [into it].' (GA 152, 7 March 1914.) Of particular importance here is the reference to the 'earthly human form', for this points towards the rescuing of the phantom—not, of course, the culmination of this process, which occurred only through the Mystery of Golgotha, but a decisive event at the time.

These three supersensible deeds of Christ also form the three stages of His approach to the Earth. 'Thus Christ gradually approached the Earth. The first and second preliminary stages were in the world of Devachan, the third was in the astral world and the event of Golgotha in the physical world.' (GA 152, 30 March 1914.) These three deeds can from a cosmological point of view be brought into connection with the following cosmic spheres: the first deed was brought about out of the starry aspect of the Sun and is therefore associated with the entire zodiac; the second took place out of its planetary aspect, where it is connected as the leader of all the forces of the planets that encircle it. And the third deed came about out of the immediate vicinity of the Earth, which in the cosmos corresponds to the Moon sphere.

From what has been said there emerges a mighty picture which reveals the whole cosmic and earthly dimension of the present Second Coming. At the centre of world evolution is the Mystery of Golgotha, which has taken place on Earth as a unique and unrepeatable event. It was preceded by three cosmic preliminary stages. They are mirrored by the three 'subsequent stages', of which Christ's appearance in the etheric is the first. In the present age of Michael this has as its mirror-picture a particular relationship to the last preliminary stage, in which as we have already seen the being of Michael took an important part. Thus when we consider the present appearance of Christ in the etheric we must always maintain its connection with the cosmic dimension of this event as briefly sketched here: the Mystery of Golgotha in the middle; its three cosmic preliminary stages; and the three ensuing spiritual revelations of Christ of which the first is taking place in our time. And just as the three preliminary stages signify at the same time the path of Christ's approach to the Earth, so are His three revelations after the Mystery of Golgotha also stages where— together with mankind—He will ascend to ever higher regions of the spiritual world.[2]

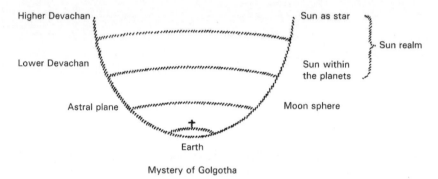

Mystery of Golgotha

At this point a further question arises: what is the relationship of the entelechy of Jesus of Nazareth—once he had passed with Christ through the Mystery of Golgotha—to the further life of the Risen One in the spiritual surroundings of the Earth and to His present manifestation in etheric form? Rudolf Steiner gives a clear answer to this question as well. In order to understand it properly, however, a further aspect of the working of this entelechy must be considered.

Even though the sister soul of Adam had never incarnated on Earth before the Turning Point of Time, it did on one occasion come so close to earthly events that Rudolf Steiner was even able to speak of a kind of incorporation or 'substitute embodiment' (GA 142, 1 January 1913). This came about in the appearance of Krishna—as a single pre-Christian revelation of the Adam soul kept safely in heaven—directly on Earth. And what happened to this Adamic or Krishna being after Christ's Resurrection? It formed the soul- or astral sheath for the Risen One. Rudolf Steiner describes this in connection with Paul's vision before the gate of Damascus. For what was manifested there consisted of two parts. In the centre was the form of Christ, surrounded by a mighty aura of light which, according to Rudolf Steiner's spiritual research, was the being of

Krishna. 'When Paul had his vision before Damascus, what appeared to him was the Christ. But the light-filled radiance in which Christ was arrayed was Krishna.' (Ibid.) And there now follow the decisive words in this respect, that 'Christ has taken Krishna as His own soul-sheath, *through which He then proceeds to work*' (ibid.).[3]

As has been stated elsewhere, Paul's experience before Damascus has a particular relationship to the present possibilities of perceiving the etheric Christ. Hence in many lectures Rudolf Steiner referred to Paul's experience again and again as an important paradigm, by which is meant that Christ in His Second Coming continues to work, just as He did in Paul's vision in the light-filled soul-sheath of Krishna or the sister soul of Adam.

This is also attested in the proclamation of the Second Coming by Theodora in the first mystery play *The Portal of Initiation* (GA 14). Before the eye of the seeress there first appears the form of the etheric Christ, speaking of Himself in the first person ('I lived . . .'), whereupon 'a human being' comes forth from the shining light that surrounds His form who speaks of Christ in the third person, as though bearing witness of Him and of His life at the Turning Point of Time. This scene is indicative of the direct participation of the entelechy of Jesus of Nazareth in Christ's Second Coming.[4] And it is obvious that this participation will continue to exist also in the course of His two further supersensible revelations, for these will manifest themselves in human evolution as the spiritual mirror-pictures of the first two preliminary stages of the Mystery of Golgotha, in which the sister soul of Adam played so significant a part.

That in his research into the cosmic dimension of the Mystery of Golgotha, with its three preliminary stages, Rudolf Steiner made a particular inner connection to Paul and his Damascus experience becomes clearly apparent from the end of the lecture in which, on one single occasion, he brought the preliminary stages and his research from the Fifth Gospel into a single focus. The passage in question, where Rudolf Steiner's method of research is also addressed, runs as follows: 'For in that Paul's vision was extended from the Mystery of Golgotha to its three preliminary stages, in that it was extended from what Paul conceived of as being virtually only a perception of Jesus of Nazareth to the life of Christ Jesus, Paul's method of investigation is broadened from a single centre to the whole vast phenomenon of the life of Christ Jesus. If in this way we can, through dedicated occult research, enter into a situation where we can truly apply the Pauline method to a knowledge of Christ, a real step forward will have been taken in the knowledge of Christ.' (GA 152, 27 May 1914.)[5]

It is a deeply founded spiritual reality that in these words about researching the preliminary stages of the Mystery of Golgotha Paul is particularly emphasized. For, as we have already seen, in his Damascus vision he experienced the supersensible collaboration of Christ and the sister soul of Adam,[6] which had already come about three times in the spiritual worlds and continued to exist also after the Mystery of Golgotha until Christ's present manifestation in the etheric, of which Paul's experience represents a kind of model. In this sense, what is referred to in the words quoted above as the 'Pauline method' is alone suitable to expand knowledge of the Mystery of Golgotha from 'a single centre' to the three preliminary and the three subsequent stages, so as to manifest the Christ event in the whole of its cosmic significance.[7]

It was this step in the form of a direct further development of the Pauline method of research, where the Christ mystery—as with the event of Damascus—was investigated in the light of and with the collaboration of the sister soul of Adam, that Rudolf Steiner took through anthroposophy. This is why, at the end of this unique lecture where his insights into the cosmic preliminary stages of the Mystery of Golgotha were united with his research on the Fifth Gospel, he could say with complete justification: 'The occult science of our day puts us in the position of knowing more and at a deeper level about Christ Jesus than previous centuries have known. So we may say that the form of Christ grows to cosmic proportions when we try to get to know it with the means that modern occultism places at our disposal.' (Ibid.) And in this particular case this happened as a further application of the 'Pauline method'.

In that Rudolf Steiner extended the understanding of Christ and research into His Being to the entire spiritual cosmos and its various realms, it became possible for him to speak about the present appearance of Christ in the etheric in such a way that the cosmic dimension of this event also becomes clearly apparent from his research: 'Thus the great, mighty event of Christ's appearance in the etheric will have significance *for all worlds*' (GA 118, 10 May 1910). Moreover, this cosmic dimension embraces not only all the various realms of the spiritual world but also the hierarchic beings who are active there.

Thus there are two aspects of Christ's Second Coming in the etheric that need to be distinguished. At its central focus is Christ's actual appearance in the spiritual world, surrounded by various helping influences from other beings. One of these helping influences has already been spoken about—the entelechy of Jesus of Nazareth, which forms the light-filled astral sheath for the etheric Christ. Another and still higher being—one who already belongs to the hierarchies—creates the etheric sheath for the etheric Christ. This being enters mightily into view at the end of the cycle on the folk-souls and is known in Nordic mythology as Vidar. Rudolf Steiner spoke about him as follows in the last lecture of this cycle: 'These future powers, however, are known to Nordic mythology; it is fully aware of their existence. It knows that the etheric form exists in which shall be embodied what we shall see again as the etheric form of Christ.' (GA 121, 17 June 1910.) And then in this context he went on to speak expressly of Vidar. For what follows it is also of significance that this etheric engirdling in the spiritual world is directly connected with the being of love. For Rudolf Steiner also refers to the etheric body as the 'body of love' (GA 130, 2 December 1911).

Christ's appearance in the etheric has, of course, nothing to do with a physical sheath, as was available to Him at the Turning Point of Time, but is related to something which has a considerable place in the spiritual world. A spiritual domain must be created here for the etheric Christ in which He can appear to mankind in a pure imagination undistorted by the adversarial powers. Rudolf Steiner describes this in the following words: 'This event of Christ's manifestation . . . can be brought about only if Michael's rulership extends to an ever greater extent. This is an ongoing process in the spiritual world. It is as though on the plane that borders upon our world Michael is battling for the approach of Christ . . . Michael must wage the battle that I have indicated so that He does not appear in a false form, in a subjective human imagination, but in a true aspect.' (GA 158, 9 November 1914.)

What is of great significance in the words that have been quoted is Rudolf Steiner's observation that the etheric appearance of Christ in our time is directly associated with the extension of Michael's rulership. It follows from this that Christ's Second Coming in the etheric can be noticed and also rightly understood by human beings only if in the next two centuries (the duration of Michael's present rulership over mankind) the Michael impulse pervades Western civilization.

From this it becomes clear why in the later years of his life Rudolf Steiner spoke far more about Michael than about Christ. In the present Michael age the path to Christ should be followed only in accordance with the Time Spirit, that is, in accordance with Michael, who goes before Christ in order to lead human beings to Him. In the spiritual world this is *already* the case. It must now also become a reality amongst human beings on Earth. This means in effect the earthly fulfilment of what Rudolf Steiner describes for the spiritual world in the following words: 'In our time it is Michael's task to become more and more the being who serves Christ; so that the statement that Michael's rulership enters into human destiny as a predominant element also means that it is true to say that Christ's sovereignty will extend over the Earth. One could say that Michael carries in advance the light of spiritual knowledge, while at the rear Christ bears the demands of universal human love.' (GA 218, 19 November 1922.) It follows from this that the true sovereignty of Christ on Earth can begin only if, as a Michaelic impulse, 'spiritual knowledge'—that is, modern spiritual science or anthroposophy—extends its sway amongst mankind so as to enable the etheric Christ to work rightly and effectively within it. (See further regarding this in the second chapter.) Thus Michael is active on the Earth today as a power 'who leads man towards the Christ on the true path of salvation'.[8]

All this can be summarized thus. From a cosmic standpoint, the etheric Christ as He appears in our time has a threefold web of garments. From the former Jesus being He receives the astral sheath, from Vidar the etheric and from Michael the physical space where He can manifest Himself to human beings in an undistorted form.[9] Likewise in a temporal perspective, these three beings who accompany the Christ and serve Him will play a decisive part in the future. The sister soul of Adam is above all connected with His etheric Second Coming; Vidar will also participate in His second, astral manifestation; and Michael will at a still more distant point in the future, when the Earth is preparing for its reunion with the Sun, collaborate in the revelation of Christ as the World Ego.

★

Out of his spiritual research Rudolf Steiner refers to another kind of sheath formation for the Christ Being. This has to do not with the collaborative influence of supersensible beings but with that of human beings themselves. This process has to be concluded by the end of earthly evolution, so that Christ can be united with mankind to form a unified organism. Vladimir Solovyov refers to this organism as the future 'God-manhood' or 'divine humanity'.[10] In order to attain this goal, human beings must through morally working upon themselves develop above all three qualities in their souls, whence the three supersensible sheaths for the Christ Being can then arise. The first, the astral sheath, emerges from all feelings of wonder (astonishment) and devotion towards the spiritual in man and in life.[11] The second, etheric sheath is formed out of all impulses of love and compassion. And from all deeds that follow the stirrings of conscience a kind of physically based supersensible sheath is brought into being which forges for Christ the inner space in which He can be active amongst mankind as its new group Ego. 'Thus the future evolution of mankind will be brought about through the collaboration between the moral impulses of human beings and the Christ impulse. We see mankind in perspective before us like a great organic structure. When people understand how to merge their actions with this great organism, to weave their impulses around it like a sheath by means of their deeds, they will in the course of earthly evolution lay the foundations for a great community which can be fully pervaded, fully imbued, by the Christ impulse.' (GA 155, 30 May 1912.)

The great future perspective—encompassing the entire second half of earthly evolution—described in these words must begin to come to manifestation in the present period, that is, at the time when Christ is beginning to appear in the etheric realm. For when a person turns consciously today to the spiritual world and forms a relationship to it in the pure mood of wonder and reverence, he will be helping the entelechy of Krishna-Jesus to enable the astral light-aura around the Christ to become ever stronger and more radiant. And if human beings offer up their selfless love to the spirit whom through spiritual science they have recognized in all the beings and other entities around them, they can strengthen the etheric sheath that Vidar fashions today for the Christ. Moreover, through all deeds that they carry out today from their forces of conscience, which in the years to come will increasingly be transformed into the capacity to behold karma or destiny (see chapter 4), people will be collaborating in the forming of the spiritual sphere around the etheric Christ, which is the aim of Michael's activity today in the world bordering upon the Earth.

In words that were quoted earlier Rudolf Steiner indicates that 'Michael's rulership enters into human destiny as a predominant element', which is a reference to the fact that Michael is directly associated today with this transformation of conscience into the beholding of karma. In the same lecture he gives a striking example of such a compensatory activity on the part of man which springs from his sharing in the experience of the influence of Michael and Christ in the period before birth and at the same time offers a mighty perspective of the moral development of mankind. He indicates that in future—but beginning in our present Michael epoch—a person will become able immediately before birth to sacrifice the physical body that has been prepared for him to another human being to whom he owes a significant karmic debt from previous earthly lives, and himself to incarnate in this other person's body.

Rudolf Steiner then goes on to indicate in a few words that in a still more distant future, 'when the Earth has itself made the transition to other states of being', people will also mysteriously exchange their souls. 'And in the course of earthly incarnations it will begin to arise that through these mutual endeavours in the spiritual domain we will be preparing for a future time ... when the souls of human beings will even while on Earth be able to enter into the bodies of those to whom they have done some special hurt, and *to receive the other soul into their own body*' (GA 218, 19 November 1922).

Christ Himself referred to this future time in St John's Gospel, where He calls such a deed one of the highest love: 'Greater love has no man than this, that a man lay down his soul[12] for his friends' (15:13). In the Russian translation it says 'his soul' here, whereas Luther and Emil Bock use the rendering 'his life'. However, both variants have a deeper meaning. For between the time when souls can be exchanged and our time, when this comes to be possible with bodies, there lies an in-between period in which a comparable exchanging of etheric bodies ('his life') can come about.

These three sacrificial steps have a direct inner relationship with the three revelations of Christ described in this chapter. In His etheric form He will, as the Lord of Karma, give man the power to make a free resolve to sacrifice his physical body. Out of the power of the second revelation a person will in future derive the strength to place 'his life'—that is, his etheric body—at the disposal of another human being. And in the light of the third, highest revelation of Christ in His Ego, the individual human ego will be imbued to such an extent with the Christ impulse that also the third sacrifice, that of his soul, will be possible for him. For only through this threefold sacrificial path on the part of human beings, of which Christ's deed in the Mystery of Golgotha stands as the highest archetype, will the Earth be able to find its true fulfilment. Mankind will then be able to live on as a karmic whole, imbued with Christ as its new group Ego. Through this mutual balancing out of karma amongst human beings their moral development will be so accelerated that the ultimate purpose of the Earth in conjunction with Christ can be achieved. 'The Earth could never attain its goal if this were not to happen; humanity would never otherwise be able to become a whole. And this must come about!' (GA 218, 19 November 1922.) Thus through the three supersensible revelations of Christ His activity as the Lord of Karma will come to fulfilment. 'In truth, this is something that begins in the twentieth century [with Christ's appearance in the etheric] and continues until the end of the Earth. The judgement—that is, the ordering of karma—begins from our twentieth century onwards.' (GA 130, 2 December 1911.)

Thus one can see that, as people of our time, we lend strength to Christ's appearance in the etheric when, by developing within ourselves the three moral qualities that have been mentioned, we help the sister soul of Adam, Vidar and Michael to form and strengthen the sheaths for the etheric Christ. In this way, through our help and service we become the conscious collaborators of these spiritual beings in the etheric Second Coming, the most important supersensible event of our time.

This also has a direct relationship to the event of a person's encounter with the etheric Christ in the present. When He appears before one's inner vision one can but respond with the three soul impulses that have been referred to. As one perceives the radiant aura of light around the etheric Christ the first impulse of one's soul is to respond with a feeling of the deepest *wonder* and reverence. For this appearance of Christ is the greatest miracle of our time. And if from the midst of this radiant aura the majestic form of Christ Himself comes forth, one will then sense the second impulse in one's soul, that of the strongest *love* towards this etheric manifestation, with which alone a person can respond to the boundless love bestowed upon him by Christ when He meets him. This then leads to the third soul impulse, which now embraces the will forces. For this meeting would lead one to want to bring a wholly transformative energy to life, to do something completely different. However, this can only be accomplished through deeds that are in harmony with one's *conscience* and can be gradually brought about by what will develop from conscience in terms of karmic vision. Through such deeds a person becomes the collaborator of Christ as the Lord of Karma. He is then an active contributor to the world's aims.[13]

And if at this point we recall that, of all human virtues and moral qualities, love is the highest and most all-embracing,[14] we shall also find these three soul qualities in the fourth part of the Foundation Stone Meditation, where they appear as the three rays of light of the Sun of Christ:

O Light Divine,[15] O Sun of Christ!	The source of all moral qualities
Warm Thou Our Hearts,	*Love*
Enlighten Thou Our Heads,	*Wonder* (devotion)
That good may become What from our Hearts we would found And from our Heads direct With single purpose.	Acting out of *conscience*, which becomes karmic vision. It encompasses the forces of hearts and heads and imbues them with a new faculty of will.

(GA 260)

Why is Christ's present revelation in the etheric so intimately connected with the development of the three moral qualities referred to amongst mankind? This is so because they belong inseparably to Christ Himself. And since from the very outset He has embodied them to the fullest extent in Himself and represented them with His entire Being, they also become visible in His outward manifestation. In the features of His face He indelibly bears the characteristics of these three qualities. Hence Rudolf Steiner describes Christ's countenance as consisting of these aspects: in the brow is revealed the highest reverence for the divine mysteries of existence; from the eyes there radiates the strongest power of love and compassion; and the form of the mouth and chin give expression to a pure revelation of cosmic conscience.

Rudolf Steiner summarized this description in the following sentence, addressing as he did so the future artist who was to try to paint a true image of Christ in accordance with these indications: 'This will have to be a head that it would not be possible to encounter amongst physical humanity' (GA 133, 14 May 1912). This is a reference to the supersensible image of Christ which only a few years later Rudolf Steiner executed with his own hands in the central motif of the First Goetheanum and in the sculptural Group. It follows from this that if a person would seek to encounter Christ in *this* form as a supersensible Being, that is, in His etheric form, he must have developed these three moral qualities within himself, in order to bring them into His presence. For like can only be perceived and also recognized by like.

To summarize, one can say that these three moral qualities—wonder, love (the greatest of the three) and conscience, all of which have their origin in the Being of Christ[16]—must be developed by man in accordance with the threefold aim of the evolution of mankind. By the end of the Earth aeon the three sheaths for Christ as the Ego of all humanity need to have been fashioned. And at the time of the Second Coming in the etheric human beings can contribute their help to supersensible beings in the course of this event. It is above all the development of the three qualities referred to that leads in our time to man's being able consciously to encounter the etheric Christ in the spiritual world bordering upon the Earth.

In this way spiritual science forms a mighty arch from the cosmic dimension of Christ's Second Coming to His appearance in the individual life of man, the central event of a person's inner biography.

★

To conclude, the following brief calculation can be made as a means of calling to mind a further aspect of Christ's future revelations. If one assumes that the second supersensible revelation of Christ—that is, His appearance in the astral body on the plane of Lower Devachan—will last as long as the first, i.e. 3000 years, the end of this time will be reached in the year 8000 (2000 + 3000 + 3000 = 8000).

According to Rudolf Steiner this will be the time when the Moon will reunite with the Earth. Mankind will then pass through the greatest test with regard to the forces of evil, which will be enormously strengthened on Earth once this reunion has taken place. The second supersensible revelation of Christ will help human beings to withstand this test and turn the Moon forces into powers of goodness. Equally, it will make a decisive contribution in surmounting the trials of the War of All against All, which will take place at the end of the seven post-Atlantean cultural epochs,[17] and, hence, in introducing the next great period of Earth evolution (the sixth).

After the catastrophe of the War of All against All, mankind will in the sixth great period of Earth evolution—once it has withstood the union with the Moon—be prepared for the union with the Sun. The third supersensible revelation of Christ will especially serve this end. Appearing in the full glory of His World Ego in Higher Devachan, Christ will prepare human beings and lead the Earth to union with the Sun.

As in our time the diffusion of ego consciousness into the spiritual world brings about an encounter with the etheric Christ, at the time of the union of the Earth with the Moon mankind will take hold of its higher ego, in order through the connection with the astral Christ to withstand the great temptation of the Moon forces and lead the evolution of humanity forth through the great catastrophe of the War of All against All. In the sixth great period, finally, the connection with the true ego becomes possible.[18] This will be the time when the spiritualization of all life's circumstances will be fully in process. Then the Christ as the World Ego will also join forces with man's true ego, in order to lead mankind to Sun existence.

Thus the three supersensible revelations of Christ encompass the whole future evolution of the Earth extending to its total spiritualization and final union with the Sun as the cosmic home of the Christ Himself. One can therefore say that through these three stages Christ will raise earthly humanity into His cosmic kingdom and, hence, bring the present Earth aeon to an end.

2. The Appearance of Christ in the Etheric and the Being Anthroposophia

In 1917, which was a momentous year for the whole of human evolution, Rudolf Steiner referred in Berlin to the fact that an initiate could perceive Christ's arrival in the etheric world already from 1909 onwards (see GA, 6 February 1917), an event which would also be accessible to the rest of humanity 21 years later.

From 1910 onwards Rudolf Steiner began to speak with great intensity of how the most important task of anthroposophy in our time is the *proclaiming* of this event and the *preparation* of mankind for it.[1] No power on Earth or in heaven can prevent the appearance of Christ in itself. However, it is the aim of the opposing forces that His revelation shall pass by unnoticed by human beings.

This is why the proclaiming of this event through anthroposophy is of such significance. Rudolf Steiner spoke about it until the very end of his lecturing activity in September 1924.[2] He also expressed this theme artistically in the first mystery play, *The Portal of Initiation* (1910), and brought it to public attention in book form in 1911.[3]

The whole of anthroposophy can actually be regarded as a preparation for this event. For it is the modern path of initiation which enables man to enter the spiritual world bordering upon the Earth through the transforming and spiritualizing of human thinking. It is also the path to the experiencing of conscious imaginations, which can be beheld by human beings through the new organ of perception of their transformed thinking. In this sense Rudolf Steiner speaks of the 'intellectual' clairvoyance which must be attained in order to perceive the etheric Christ in the present Michael epoch. He says in this regard: 'Progress will be made in this direction only if people develop a heightened intellectuality not merely for themselves but also bear it aloft into the astral world' (GA 130, 18 November 1911). However, this is possible only if human individuals are able to transform their intellect into a new faculty by working intensively with spiritual science and, hence, *observe* the essential nature of an idea, in order thereby to take the decisive step from experiencing thoughts to beholding imaginations. Then such imaginations will be imbued from the outset with the same clarity and intensity of consciousness as one otherwise knows only from one's thought life.

Rudolf Steiner has more to say about this in the same lecture: 'Through

such *a development towards intellectual clairvoyance*, the etherically visible
Christ can and will approach a person who has advanced in this way more
and more clearly over the course of the next three thousand years' (ibid.).
It is for this reason that the transforming and spiritualizing of thinking
plays so central a role in anthroposophy. Ordinary, deductive reasoning,
which consists only of abstract conceptualizing, must as a first step be
transformed into a new 'creative, formative thinking' [*gestaltende Denken*]
which has a sense-free origin and is therefore to a large extent independent of the physical body. This kind of intuitive, visionary thinking
[*anschauende Denken*] also lived in germinal form in Goethe. Hence
Rudolf Steiner, following Goethe, also calls it 'morphological thinking'.
(See GA 79, 26 November 1921.) The whole of Goetheanism is based on
this thinking and can be developed further only on this foundation.
Nevertheless, the developmental potential of thinking goes far beyond
this; and the book *Knowledge of Higher Worlds* gives an indication of these
significant possibilities.[4]

Creative, formative thinking acquires a purely imaginative expression—where thinking has been raised to Imagination—in the artistic
forms of the First Goetheanum. Rudolf Steiner gives an indication of this
in the following words: 'If, on the other hand, you exercise creative,
formative thinking, thinking that allows for metamorphosis, I could also
say Goethean thinking, represented, for instance, in the shaping of our
pillars and capitals [in the First Goetheanum] and elsewhere; if you
exercise a thinking of this nature such is also exemplified in all the books
that I have tried to contribute to spiritual science, this thinking is closely
bound up with man' (GA 187, 1 January 1919). In this sense, all the books
from *The Philosophy of Freedom* onwards,[5] and also all the forms and their
metamorphoses in the first building, were forged by their creator out of
formative thinking, behind which, however—as we shall see—a still
higher, third kind of thinking is active in a hidden way.

In the same lecture, Rudolf Steiner presents this transition from
ordinary to formative thinking in a wider, world-encompassing perspective, which is associated with a particular event in the spiritual world.
This has to do with the fact that in our time the Spirits of Form, who are
the actual creators of Earth evolution in its entirety, have handed over the
guidance of earthly affairs to the Spirits of Personality, who are now
becoming creative in their own right. However, the whole authority of
modern intellectualism is associated with the dominion of the Exusiai, for
as Spirits of *Form* they have endowed the thinking of people of today with
the immense formalizing power that underlies the whole of present-day
civilization. The ahrimanic spirits or spirits of darkness are also involved in

this cosmic process. (See GA 286, 20 December 1918.) They are trying to make use of this withdrawal of the Exusiai from the guidance of certain earthly affairs in order to occupy the field which has become untenanted. Their particular aim in this respect is to bind human beings to purely intellectual, abstract thinking in order to prevent their further evolution under the guidance of the new creators, the Spirits of Personality. For these beings want to enter into a relationship with human beings in a completely new and free way, which is why they must wait until human individuals have themselves established the conditions for a collaboration with them through a conscious cultivation of formative thinking. Once this has been accomplished, thinking itself becomes intuitive or imaginative. This means that human beings have out of their freedom elevated thinking to an imaginative stage and, as a result, their spiritualized intellectuality to the astral plane bordering upon the Earth, where the encounter with Christ in His etheric form will then take place.[6]

It follows from what has been said that the study of spiritual science, the first stage of modern initiation (see GA 13) where formative thinking is to be developed, plays a decisive role from the outset. For through the inner comprehending and experiencing of anthroposophical thoughts, if they are apprehended not only with the head but also with heart-forces, a person will gradually be led towards a conscious encounter with the Christ Being.

What has been said here is further confirmed in the lecture *The Etherization of the Blood* (GA 130, 1 October 1911). There Rudolf Steiner describes how in man two streams of etherized blood are constantly rising from the region of the heart to the head and out into the spiritual surroundings. The first is the stream of the etherized blood of the human individual himself, the second that of Christ. Since the Mystery of Golgotha this second stream can be found on Earth in every human being. Rudolf Steiner characterizes the first stream as one in which 'the intellectual element streams upwards from below in the form of currents of light when a person is awake'. Because of this it is associated with the human intellect and also with the possibility of transforming it into formative thinking.

And now comes the decisive point in this connection. Man has to unite these two streams in himself, for only if they are united does it become possible to perceive Christ on the astral plane. This can happen above all through acquiring spiritual-scientific knowledge about the Christ Being and the Mystery of Golgotha, that is, through the study of anthroposophy. 'But the evolution of humanity progresses, and in our present age what matters is that people should recognize the need for the knowledge contained in spiritual science and gradually bring the fire of inspiration to what streams from the heart to the head so that it furnishes an understanding of anthroposophy. The consequence of this will be that individuals will be able to receive and comprehend the event that has its beginning in the twentieth century, which is the appearance of the etheric Christ as opposed to the physical Christ of Palestine' (ibid.). Thus through the study of anthroposophy the spiritualization of the human intellect is confirmed as being of central importance.

In 1917 Rudolf Steiner added the inspirative element of hearing as a third stage to these first two stages, the cognitive understanding and the imaginative perceiving of the etheric Second Coming. Here he refers to the whole of the anthroposophy which he founded as a *new language*, in which people today can pose such questions as they may have about the important concerns of life directly to the etheric Christ, who will then also give an answer to them. 'Through the language—however removed from our everyday experience it may seem—through which we hear about Saturn, Sun, Moon and Earth and of various periods and times and various other mysteries of earthly evolution,[7] through this so-called teaching we are teaching ourselves a language in which we can phrase the questions that we are asking of the spiritual world. And if we learn inwardly to speak rightly in the language of this spiritual life, it . . . will come about that Christ will stand by us and give us an answer.' (GA 175, 6 February 1917.)

We may best understand these words if we bear in mind that anthroposophical cosmology describes the arising and evolution of the world in such a way that it was created by the cosmic Word through the mediation of the nine hierarchies. Thus a knowledge of this creation leads a person who has made a deep inner connection with it to an intimate dialogue with the cosmic Word, with 'the Logos, as lived by Christ here on Earth among human beings'.[8] Hence Rudolf Steiner was able to indicate that the study of spiritual science does not only lead a person into the sphere of activity of the etheric Christ through the transformation of his thinking but also creates the possibility of inwardly deepening this study in such a way that the object of study (anthroposophy) becomes a new language in which a human individual can have a dialogue with Christ. From this it is clear that *Rudolf Steiner's language* belongs not to the past but to the present and above all to the future and will have full validity throughout the epoch of the etheric Second Coming (the next three thousand years).[9] Thus in this sense and from this perspective there can be no question of Rudolf Steiner's language becoming out of date but, rather, of our diminishing capacity to learn the language of the etheric Christ.

Rudolf Steiner concludes the passage quoted earlier with the following question: 'Why do we concern ourselves with spiritual science? It is as if we are to learn the vocabulary of that language through which we approach the Christ. So let us seek to acquire a relationship to spiritual science not merely as a teaching but as a language and then wait until we find the questions in this language that we may address to Christ. He will answer, yes, He *will* answer!' (Ibid., italics Rudolf Steiner.) This is the third, inspirative stage of the relationship of the etheric Christ with anthroposophy.

The fourth stage, which is also an inherent part of the process of the spiritual-scientific deepening of the new Christ event, takes the development further. Rudolf Steiner spoke about this somewhat earlier, at Christmas 1914 in Dornach. This has to do with the deepest task of anthroposophy, which must henceforth be implemented by those people who have a relationship to it: *anthroposophy must itself become the spiritual sheath in which the etheric Christ can be embodied.* Rudolf Steiner speaks about this in the following words: 'Let us nurture in our souls the confidence that what we experience today as the child whom we want to worship— this child being the new understanding of Christ [in anthroposophy]— will grow, will live, and will in a relatively short time advance to the point where the etherically appearing Christ can incarnate within it, just as Christ was able to incarnate in bodily substance at the time of the Mystery of Golgotha' (GA 156, 26 December 1914). These words are indicative of the greatest mystery associated with the being Anthroposophia and her task in the age of the etheric Second Coming.

If from this standpoint one considers the relationship of the being Anthroposophia to anthroposophists, one can discover the same four stages as have been indicated here with respect to this being. Almost two years previously, on 3 February 1913, Rudolf Steiner had devoted an entire lecture to this being and its development at the first General Assembly of the Anthroposophical Society since it became independent from the Theosophical Society (the final separation took place at Christmas 1912). The path of this mysterious being led through the whole cultural development of mankind from ancient Greece through the Middle Ages to the present.[10] As theosophy (divine Sophia), philosophy and anthroposophy this being has manifested itself to many of the most outstanding spirits of those epochs, exemplified by such names as Aristotle at the time of the high-point of Greek culture, Thomas Aquinas in the Christian Middle Ages and Rudolf Steiner, the creator of anthroposophy in the twentieth century.

Through the study of anthroposophy we too can approach this being.

The process culminates in that once a person has taken up anthroposophy with sufficient intensity he can come to experience it as a real spiritual being, as a true Anthroposophia. This being then stands before him in the spiritual world bordering upon the Earth as a living imagination and leads to true self-knowledge appropriate to the epoch of the consciousness or spiritual soul. 'She will appear before him objectively, now no longer simply as "Sophia" but as "Anthroposophia", as that Sophia who, after she has passed through the human soul [in the course of studying spiritual science], through man's being, now bears this being of man within herself and henceforth manifests herself before one who seeks knowledge as in former times did Sophia, that objective being who was known to the Greeks ... For this is the essence of anthroposophy, that its own being consists of what man's being consists' (ibid.). For Anthroposophia will appear before man's imaginative gaze as a real being of the spiritual world, so that he perceives 'the reflection of his being in her as the fruit of true self-knowledge in anthroposophy' (ibid.).

Ten years later Rudolf Steiner again focused upon this imaginative relationship with Anthroposophia in the process of self-knowledge; this was in lectures that he gave in the summer of 1923, where he was beginning to prepare anthroposophists for the coming Christmas Conference with a great review of the history of the anthroposophical movement. In the lecture-cycle significantly entitled 'The History and Conditions of the Anthroposophical Movement in relation to the Anthroposophical Society' (GA 258), he spoke of the decisive 'condition of the life' of the Anthroposophical Society which must now be fulfilled by its members for the Society's further existence: 'to regard anthroposophy as a living being' (16 June 1923). For 'anthroposophy is in itself an invisible human being who goes amongst visible human beings and towards whom we have the greatest conceivable responsibility' (ibid.).[11]

In the same lecture Rudolf Steiner adds the next, inspirative stage to this imaginative aspect of the meeting with Anthroposophia, who remains invisible to physical eyes but can be experienced supersensibly through a thinking that has risen to being able to apprehend the world of imaginations in the manner described. Thus he speaks in virtually the same words as in 1917 about the etheric Christ, about this being who 'must indeed be regarded as *an invisible human being*, as someone with a real existence, who should be consulted in all life's individual actions' (ibid.).

Still later, in the November of the same year, during his stay in The Hague on the occasion of the founding of the Dutch National Society, Rudolf Steiner touched on this theme anew and above all developed the inspirative stage of this process. What he said there acquired a particular

weight through the fact that during this stay in Holland he finally decided
to hold the Christmas Conference. Thus the address that he gave there
made it apparent that he had arrived at a final resolution in this connection
after an intensive spiritual consultation with this being.[12]

The inspirative element with regard to anthroposophy was now
expressed with even greater intensity than five months before and then
led over into the intuitive element; for here it was no longer a question of
hearing the being Anthroposophia but of uniting oneself with her within
one's own heart. An individual may now receive Anthroposophia directly
into his heart. Thus she no longer appears to him as an invisible human
being but as the 'living being of worlds'. As such this being approaches our
soul, knocks 'at the portals of our heart ... and says: Let me in, for I am
you yourself, I am your true human nature'.[13] In this way the human
individual is united with anthroposophy in his heart in an intuitive
relationship.

That in this case an intuitive relationship is indeed being manifested
here is clear from the fact that anthroposophy becomes the source of
spiritual love within the human heart. 'When we let anthroposophy into
our hearts once it has knocked, anthroposophy brings us—through what
it is in its essential nature—true human love' (ibid.), that is, that power of
brotherly love with which alone a human community that serves this
being can remain firmly connected with it on Earth. Hence Rudolf
Steiner repeatedly emphasizes that true brotherliness has a great significance for all spiritual communities, but for the Anthroposophical
Society in particular it is of an absolute binding necessity. 'Anthroposophy
demands quite explicitly true human brotherliness down to the very
depths of the soul. In other words one can say: brotherliness is an absolute
requirement. Where anthroposophy is concerned one must say: it grows
only on the ground of brotherliness, it cannot prosper except in a state of
brotherliness.' (GA 211, 11 June 1922.) For only on the basis of a
brotherliness derived from true spiritual love can the relationship of a
community of human beings to this supersensible being survive.

In other words, if a person is to be inwardly imbued, and have an
intuitive relationship, with Anthroposophia, this is only possible if he has
the deepest possible love towards her. Through her entry into the human
heart she becomes a new, creative social impulse. Love itself is in this case
the power that makes a person intuitively aware and, hence, establishes an
ever deeper and more existential relationship with the being Anthroposophia. As exemplified in the following words, Rudolf Steiner spoke
repeatedly about the relationship that one can have to the capacity for
love—the highest cognitive power that a person possesses—which

enables one to have an intimate connection with the object of cognition, a process which corresponds to spiritual communion: 'What is revealed through Intuition can be attained only by developing and spiritualizing to the highest degree the capacity for love. A person must be able to make this capacity for love into a cognitional force.' (GA 227, 20 August 1923.)

This theme of man's inner connection with the being Anthroposophia was shortly afterwards taken further by Rudolf Steiner during the Christmas Conference and, on 25 December 1923, at the laying of the foundation stone of the newly founded General Anthroposophical Society, before the members present, put forward as its new task. Now each of them was inwardly to accomplish as a free deed 'the enlivening of his heart through and through by Anthroposophia' (GA 260). This is another way of expressing what Rudolf Steiner had previously described in The Hague regarding allowing this being to enter into the human heart. That he was referring to this process is also attested by the fact that both cases have to do with *self-knowledge*, which has an intrinsic relationship with Anthroposophia. (At the laying of the foundation stone the words 'O Man, know thyself' intimately pervaded everything that was taking place there.)

From all of this it is understandable why, at the beginning of his first letter to the members, which he distributed soon after the Christmas Conference to the members of the newly founded Society, Rudolf Steiner first mentions love for anthroposophy: 'The real meaning [of the Christmas Conference] will only be fulfilled if in the future, in all the world, *those who love anthroposophy* can feel that a new life has entered into anthroposophy through what was implanted there' (GA 260a, 20 January 1924). This new anthroposophical life will then flow into the Anthroposophical Society from the souls of those people who have previously opened their hearts to the being Anthroposophia in order to live inwardly in communion with her.

The second consequence is the connection of Anthroposophia with what at the laying of the foundation stone was described as the 'formative substance' of love out of which Rudolf Steiner created the foundation stone of love. Here we have a direct path from '*formative* thinking', which opens the gates into the imaginative world, to the '*formative* substance', which is brought forth from man's intuitive powers. The foundation stone created by Rudolf Steiner during the Christmas Conference can as a supersensible structure only be beheld in its imaginative form, which is why he also characterizes it as 'an imagination that has received its form through love' (GA 260, 25 December 1923). Its inner essence, or its substance, which consists of pure spiritual love, is only attainable through intuitive knowledge, that is, solely through becoming inwardly connected with this substance in one's own soul.

As is evident from what was said at the Christmas Conference, the foundation stone created out of this substance of love was given to the members as the spiritual foundation of the Anthroposophical Society. At the same time Rudolf Steiner also gave an indication of its most important spiritual task as he concluded the whole mystery-deed of the laying of the foundation stone, namely together to 'found here a true community of human beings for Anthroposophia' (ibid.). And so in a certain sense the circle is closed. What in February 1913, at the official opening of the independent Anthroposophical Society in Berlin, was placed before its members still as an *individual* task was at its transformation into the *General* Anthroposophical Society in 1923/24 given as a new *social* task, in that now, standing on the supersensible foundation stone of love, human beings might find themselves in an organization for the high spiritual being Anthroposophia.[14]

Whereas at the inauguration of the Society in 1913 the emphasis was still around the relationship with the being Anthroposophia on the individual path of self-knowledge, which has the potential capacity to lead to a conscious encounter with this being in the spiritual world, the aim of the founding of the Society in 1923 was in addition the forming of a new human community which, by standing on a common spiritual foundation, would be prepared through a spirit of brotherly love to create a social soul-spiritual sheath for a being of the higher worlds.

This also enables one to understand the esoteric significance of the fact that one of the important demands that led to the Christmas Conference was for 'more anthroposophy'. In the lecture of 25 January 1924, looking back at the Christmas Conference and his having taken over the leadership of the Anthroposophical Society which ensued from it, Rudolf Steiner said in this regard: 'Only because I believe that life in the Anthroposophical Society must become more active than it has been, only because I believe that to this end *more anthroposophy* needs to be cultivated in the Anthroposophical Society than has been the case hitherto—I do not mean in the sense of more content, but with greater intensity, more enthusiasm and love—have I decided ... to begin anew' (GA 240). It follows from these words that such an intensifying signifies above all the transformation of the relationship to anthroposophy from a teaching into an inner union with Anthroposophia as a living being of the spiritual world, which can only happen out of 'enthusiasm and love'.

Thus from what has been presented here a new perspective results with respect to the esoteric tasks and aims of the Anthroposophical Society, which emerges from the relationship of the two streams of etherized blood characterized in this chapter. We have seen that four stages can be distinguished in the etheric Second Coming which correspond precisely to those of the anthroposophical path of initiation: the study of spiritual science, Imagination, Inspiration and Intuition.

The same four stages can also be found in the relationship to anthroposophy: from studying it as a source of, and educator in, the new, formative thinking until the stage of Intuition, where it enters the human heart as Anthroposophia and establishes an intimate bond with it. At the level of Intuition everything flows together.[15] For, as we have already seen, the etheric Christ Himself will in the far future be spiritually embodied in the being Anthroposophia, in order to be received together with her into the human ego. Then Anthroposophia will be the new Grail chalice in the spiritual world, bearing Christ within herself and joining forces with human beings. Because this is so, Rudolf Steiner was enabled at the end of his book *Occult Science*, which was written in the year of the etheric appearance of Christ (1909), to characterize the whole of anthroposophy as represented by himself as the 'knowledge of the Grail' (GA 13).

Here one can find further substantiation for the deep connection of anthroposophy with the modern Grail mysteries.[16] These mysteries lead today to the goal which Rudolf Steiner characterizes in the following words: 'If souls allow spiritual science to kindle an understanding of such mysteries, if our souls can actively engage in such an understanding, they will become mature enough to recognize in that holy chalice the mystery of Christ's Ego, the eternal Ego which every human ego can become. This mystery *is* a reality. All that people have to do is to hearken to the call by spiritual science [that is, by Anthroposophia] to understand this mystery as a given fact so that as they contemplate the Holy Grail the Ego of Christ may be received into their being' (GA 109/111, 11 April 1909; italics Rudolf Steiner).[17] In the sense of these words spiritual science or anthroposophy is today the mediator between human beings and the copies of Christ's Ego preserved in the Grail vessel, which can be received by those people who seek them only on the basis of their collaboration with Christ.

As in this chapter the attempt was made to bring the etheric appearance of Christ into connection with the being Anthroposophia and the modern path of initiation, this must also be carried out with respect to all other areas of anthroposophy, including the daughter movements that have arisen from it. For in our time the etheric Christ wants to manifest Himself to human beings in all spheres of life out of His eternal *present*, and the being Anthroposophia has the task to prepare them for this in order thereby to pave the way for the etheric Christ's access to mankind.

The present task of the Anthroposophical Society emerges from this; for the relationship of anthroposophy with the etheric Christ needs to be made a living reality through the common spiritual work of its members in such a way that they are inseparably united with one another in the spiritual world. Only if this happens will the great ideal come to fulfilment in the future which resides in the final union of the two paths that have been described here. The Christ manifesting Himself in etheric form will incarnate in an Anthroposophia who has grown to maturity, that is, has reached full development, if for her part she has found the soul-spiritual sheath appropriate to her on Earth in the Anthroposophical Society, a sheath which has been prepared by its members through what has ensued from the impulse of the Christmas Conference.

★

The four stages of initiation that have been described here in connection with Christ's appearance in the etheric were artistically portrayed by Rudolf Steiner in the First Goetheanum, in its very architecture and in all its forms and colours, in such a way that every person who entered this building with unprejudiced feelings open to the spirit had the possibility of experiencing a kind of encounter with the etheric Christ.[18]

The whole form of the building was conceived as a double domed construction in such a way that it corresponded as regards its architecture to the words with which Rudolf Steiner subsequently characterized the nature of anthroposophy: 'Anthroposophy is a path of knowledge, to guide the spiritual in the human being to the spiritual in the universe' (GA 26, Leading Thought 1). In all its details the building was an artistic portrayal of the whole of anthroposophy, as it had previously been brought to expression in written form in the book *Occult Science*.

The first stage corresponded to an extensive study of anthroposophy through the art that was manifested in the First Goetheanum. Through this art the development of formative thinking was furthered, thus enabling it to make the transition to the perceiving of imaginations.

The second, imaginative stage was achieved in contemplating the great red window in the western stairwell. A human being is depicted here in whom the three lotus flowers, at the root of the nose, in the larynx and in the region of the heart, are fully developed, with the result that he has complete mastery of his etheric body.[19] This is a person who is already on the path from Imagination to Inspiration; and what is portrayed here is a process of inner development leading from the transformation of thinking in his head to the hearing of the spiritual word through the supersensible organ of the larynx and finally to the freeing of his heart from the powers of the dragon through the Michael impulse.[20] In this initial picture the whole further path through the Goetheanum is contained in germinal form; for the mighty countenance in the red window gazes from West to East, to where out of the spiritual world—which is always associated with an eastward orientation—the Christ was, as it were, to come to meet man in the form of a sculpture.

In the Great Hall the inspirative element was added to the imaginative element, which arises from the transforming of thinking through its becoming a new organ of perception in the imaginative world (the cupola paintings and themes of the coloured windows). The mighty columns, capitals and architraves in their sequence of metamorphosis, which encompass the whole of evolution as understood through anthroposophy, now began to speak to human beings in their cosmic language. This was the unique opportunity to experience anthroposophy as the modern language of the etheric Christ in artistic form. This cosmic language, which is comparable to a sort of music of the spheres, then became in the space of the small cupola an all-encompassing revelation of the cosmic Word, sounding through the twelve cosmic initiators (see GA 137, 12 June 1912), for whom the twelve special thrones at the base of the twelve columns were erected. By this means the next transition was prepared: from Inspiration to Intuition, from which realm the Christ Himself was to appear as the Representative of Humanity.

Thus at the end of the path the human individual encountered Christ in a twofold form, as a sculpture and as a painted image in the eastern part of the small cupola. The Goetheanum was conceived of as a work of art also for this encounter. In this building the whole of anthroposophy had become a visible sheath for the image of the Representative of Humanity, which was to form the spiritual and architectural forces of the building. (See GA 84, 9 April 1923.) The future etheric incarnation of Christ into the being Anthroposophia was thereby already artistically embodied and prepared.

In order to understand this process in the context of the sculptural Group still better, the following aspect needs to be considered. As though behind this work of art, one must today discover the 'new Isis' ('an actual, real new Isis') who is invisible to outer eyes but is truly present. In the lecture of 6 January 1918 in Dornach Rudolf Steiner told a 'new Osiris-Isis legend' and even characterizes his sculptural Group as a 'new Isis statue' (GA 180). 'People looked at the statue [the sculptural Group] and ... did not know that the statue was in fact only the veil for an invisible statue. But the invisible statue remained unnoticed; for this invisible statue was the new Isis of a new age.' (Ibid.) In this sense to lift the veil of the new Isis means for people today none other than to rise to the new, conscious clairvoyance with which the etheric Christ can be beheld. Thus in the sculptural Group the mystery of the inner path to an experience of the Second Coming is contained.

This is not the place to interpret this legend as a whole but merely to refer to one of its aspects.[21] For the awakening of the new Isis—not to ordinary waking consciousness but to the higher forces of the new clairvoyance—occurred because one day she received her spiritual off-spring 'in its true, its genuine form from a group of spirits that were elemental spirits of nature'. But now, endowed with the new clairvoy-ance, she could understand the full profundity of the meaning of the Logos mystery in the prologue to St John's Gospel. 'The Johannine significance of the Mystery of Golgotha arose in her', with the result that the crown that Typhon placed on her head, made 'merely of paper', became an 'actual gold crown of genuine wisdom'.

Thus this Osiris-Isis legend culminates in the new Isis's relationship with the essential nature of the Logos and with the power that has gone forth from the Mystery of Golgotha. In the further course of the lecture Rudolf Steiner indicates that the new Isis reached this higher stage of her development 'through the power of the Word which is to be regained through spiritual science'. In other words: this awakening of the new Isis to modern clairvoyance, which made it possible for her to have a deep-ened relationship to the Mystery of Golgotha and resulted in her paper crown becoming a gold crown of wisdom, came about through the forces of anthroposophy.

If at this point one asks from which elemental spirits the new Isis was able to receive her true offspring in order, in addition, to find the new clairvoyant path to the Mystery of Golgotha, it is obvious that they were the same elemental beings whom Rudolf Steiner addressed three times in the Foundation Stone Meditation; for they are the earthly witnesses to the fact that, after the Mystery of Golgotha, Christ became the new Spirit of the Earth. Moreover, these elemental spirits must today form the supersensible retinue of the etheric Christ, for they cannot otherwise be beheld by human beings. Rudolf Steiner refers to this in the following words: 'Before the Mystery of Golgotha mankind beheld and ensouled and enspirited nature. Since the Mystery of Golgotha mankind must endeavour to ensure that ensouled and enspirited nature forms the retinue of Christ, that the nature spirits are all seen as the retinue of Christ, for without Him they cannot be seen.' (GA 226, 21 May 1923.)[22]

Almost two years later Rudolf Steiner added the cosmic aspect. In the lecture of 24 December 1920 he offered his listeners the Christmas gift of a further 'new Isis legend' and linked it with an important task for anthroposophists: 'We must somehow rediscover the Isis legend, the Isis mystery, but we must form it out of Imagination for our own time' (GA 202). In both cases we have to do with the 'new Isis', but in the 1918 lecture the microcosmic, human-oriented aspect is emphasized and in the lecture of 1920 the macrocosmic aspect. However, they are connected with one another through the fact that in each variant of the legend spiritual science or anthroposophy plays a decisive role.

And then he related further how in our time, because mankind is inwardly so strongly under the influence of Ahriman (the forces of Typhon-Ahriman were mentioned), Lucifer gained full power over the 'new Isis', killed her and thrust forth her remains into the expanses of the cosmos. It is there that she must be found once again by human beings and awakened to new life. This happens through working with the inner, living cosmology which Rudolf Steiner has presented above all in his book *Occult Science*. And then he continues: 'We must be able to place before ourselves in a living way all that we have acquired through the newly found Isis, so that the whole cosmic heavens become spiritual for us again. We must understand Saturn, Sun, Moon, Earth, Jupiter, Venus and Vulcan from within.' (Ibid.) In other words, a new astronomy derived from anthroposophy in which the new Isis can resurrect must be set over and against the mechanical astronomy of today, which is symbolic of an Isis who has been killed by Lucifer. This can happen only because Rudolf Steiner himself came to this spiritual astronomy through the power of Christ in his ego: 'We must realize that through the power of the Christ we must find an inner astronomy which shows us once more the cosmos evolving and moving in the power of the spirit.' And if in this way a person will find the new, resurrected Isis, she can for her part lead him to a new understanding of the Christ Being as connected with the entire cosmos. For 'what we have lost is the knowledge, the intuitive perception, of Christ Jesus' (ibid.).

The whole description then culminates in the well-known words: 'It is not Christ that we lack; the knowledge of Christ, the Isis of Christ, the Sophia of Christ is what fails us' (ibid.). This is the task of anthroposophists—following Rudolf Steiner in finding the new Isis out of an inner deepening of spiritual science, in order with her power to encounter the etheric Christ on the path of the new clairvoyance. For at the end of the lecture Rudolf Steiner connects this new Isis, whom he also calls the 'holy Sophia', with the appearance of Christ in the etheric, which will only manifest itself amongst mankind if people have previously acquired the power of the holy Sophia. 'As the Egyptians looked from Isis to Osiris, we must learn to look again to the new Isis, to the holy Sophia. Christ will appear again in His spirit-form in the course of the twentieth century not because something purely of an external nature happens but through people finding that power which is represented by the holy Sophia' (ibid.).

However, the being who in the spiritual world holds the key to this clairvoyance-engendering Sophia power, and who for its part makes possible Christ's appearance in the etheric, is Anthroposophia. It was also she who inspired Rudolf Steiner regarding the two variants of the new Isis legend, so as to guide the inner eye of human beings at the same time to their relationship to the etheric Christ.

3. The Destiny of the Ego in the Age of the Etheric Christ

Every person who begins with the study of anthroposophy will soon notice that the mystery of the human ego stands at its centre. This mystery is one of the central questions of anthroposophical Christology and, indeed, one of the most important questions of anthroposophy.

From the standpoint of esoteric Christianity the words 'I am' from the seven 'I am' sayings in St John's Gospel are no mere grammatical formula but the true mystery-name of Christ. For in Christ we have to do with the God of the ego principle, with the World Ego Himself. Rudolf Steiner once brought this radically to expression in these words: 'The true name of Christ is "I am"; who does not know or does not understand this and calls Him by another name does not know anything about Him. "I am" is His only name.' (GA 266/1, 27 May 1909.)

The fact that the word 'Ich' in German represents the initials of Jesus Christ, as Rudolf Steiner frequently pointed out, is likewise an indication in the same direction. And in the lecture of 11 October 1911 (GA 131) he speaks of how through the Mystery of Golgotha the human ego was rescued for the whole future of world evolution. It follows from this that the riddle of the human ego has since then been deeply associated with the Christ impulse and can be solved only from this source.[1]

In the book *The Threshold of the Spiritual World* Rudolf Steiner describes especially succinctly and at the same time precisely what in later lectures he characterizes as man's 'ego organization'. The chapters of this book are divided into three parts, with a 'summary of the foregoing' appearing after each of these parts. The book therefore has a structure composed of three clear stages, with each stage characterizing a new aspect of the human ego-organization: 'man as an independent, individual being, or ego'; 'man's "other self"', which comes to expression in repeated earthly lives' and according to this definition corresponds to the higher ego;[2] and 'the true ego', which forms man's own spiritual essence.

The present time is from a spiritual standpoint characterized by the great event of Christ's appearance in etheric form on the astral plane. The question of Christ's relationship to man's threefold ego-organization arises from this and from His existential relationship to the human ego.

As a result of the Mystery of Golgotha a decisive change took place for the earthly ego, which is the greatest achievement of Earth evolution.

Since this time man has had the capacity of fully taking his ego-consciousness into the spiritual world and, hence, of entering it in full consciousness. Rudolf Steiner describes the unique influence of the Mystery of Golgotha upon the whole of human ego-development in the following words: 'That stage of human evolution which we have defined as an ascent of the soul to the realms of the spirit, which in pre-Christian times could be reached only within the Mysteries and through a certain dimming of the ego in so far as it was developed in normal human consciousness, was to receive an impulse—the fruits of which still lie, for the most part, in mankind's future—enabling a person entering the spiritual world fully to retain that ego-consciousness which in our time normally pertains only to the physical world of the senses. This advance in human evolution, made possible by the Christ event, is at the same time the greatest advance that has ever taken place or ever will take place in the evolution of the Earth and of humanity. That is, whatever else may develop in Earth evolution in this regard will simply be a further elaboration of the mighty impulse given by the Christ event.' (GA 123, 9 September 1910.)

In order that it might be able to bring about this new ego-development inaugurated by Christ in the Mystery of Golgotha independently, mankind had to await the full development of the consciousness soul and the establishing of spiritual science, which in the first instance addresses man's earthly ego. For it is with this earthly ego that his intellectuality is associated, which through its transformation into pure, sense-free thinking today on the modern path of schooling can be elevated together with ego-consciousness into the spiritual world, where the encounter with the etheric Christ takes place.

How this actually happens has already been indicated in the previous chapter. It entails a transformation of thinking such that the earthly ego dwelling within it can be borne aloft into the spiritual world. In chapter 9 of *The Philosophy of Freedom* Rudolf Steiner refers to this connection of the ego with thinking and of ego-consciousness with the bodily organization: 'Thinking, in its own essential nature, certainly contains the real "I" or ego, but it does not contain the ego-consciousness. To see this we have but to observe thinking with an open mind. The 'I' is to be found within thinking ... Ego-consciousness ... arises through the bodily organization.' (GA 4.) And then comes the decisive remark 'that ego-consciousness, once it has arisen, remains independent of the bodily organization. Once arisen, it is taken up into thinking and shares henceforth in thinking's spiritual being.' (Ibid.) It follows from this that spiritualized thinking, which finds the paths into the spiritual world, is able to take earthly ego-consciousness with it in order to connect it there with the higher ego. Thus through the transformation of thinking it is possible for a person to become clairvoyant while at the same time retaining the forces of his earthly ego.

What will in this respect be the common knowledge of mankind in the sixth cultural epoch can, in anticipation of this future, be developed already in our time through spiritual science and its path of schooling. 'While we are in the midst of the fifth post-Atlantean period, cultivating spiritual science and having more and more to contribute to an understanding of living thinking, a thinking that is becoming clairvoyant, we have at the same time to prepare for the sixth post-Atlantean period' (GA 152, 7 March 1914). But, as already mentioned, this 'thinking that is becoming clairvoyant'—if as 'formative thinking' it enters the astral world together with the earthly ego—leads there to the beholding of the etheric Christ. (See chapter 1.) This elevating of the spiritualized intellect into the astral world in order there to have a conscious encounter with the etheric Christ through man's becoming clairvoyant in his thinking is the most important deed that must be accomplished out of the earthly ego in our time.

Rudolf Steiner describes an essential aspect of this process in the lecture on the etherization of the blood already mentioned in the previous chapter. Here, too, the study of spiritual science—whereby thinking is gradually transformed out of the earthly ego—plays a decisive role. For only through the study of the anthroposophical knowledge of Christ can the union of the two streams of etherized blood, those of the human individual and Christ, take place. In order especially to emphasize the significance of earthly consciousness for the study of spiritual science, Rudolf Steiner formulates the first stage of modern initiation in the book *Occult Science* as follows: 'The study of spiritual science [is the first stage of modern initiation], where one initially avails oneself of the power of judgement that one has gained in the physical world of the senses' (GA 13).

The next step, once the human individual has taken his earthly ego across the threshold into the spiritual world, now consists in uniting it with his higher ego, or imbuing it with the power of the ego-consciousness which he has attained on the Earth. For man's higher or real ego does not at birth descend into the physical body but remains in the spiritual world bordering upon the Earth.

In his famous Bologna lecture, which he gave on 8 April 1911 at the Fourth International Philosophy Congress, Rudolf Steiner presented this fact which has such far-reaching implications for an understanding of man with unmistakable clarity: 'A cognitive theory of the future will recognize that the ego actually lies in the outer spiritual world and that the ordinary ego merely mirrors its reflection in the bodily organization'.[3]

In the lecture for his anthroposophical listeners Rudolf Steiner formulates this mystery as follows: 'This is the mystery that is so difficult to grasp, that the ego continues to remain at the point to which our memory extends. It is not changed with the body, it stays where it is. It is because of this that we always have it before us, that when we behold it it reflects our experiences back to us. The ego does not accompany our earthly wanderings ... This ego is kept back in the spiritual world' (GA 165, 19 December 1915). It is only the reflection of this ego that man experiences on the Earth as something that he generally calls his ego-consciousness; and this reflection, as we have already seen, can be taken on the path of formative thinking into the spiritual world in order there, beyond the threshold, consciously to reach the higher ego. That this is possible we owe to the Mystery of Golgotha.

What has been said here solves a problem which some anthroposophists have long been aware of in connection with The Philosophy of Freedom. It consists in the sentence from the third chapter: 'I can never observe my present thinking ... I can only accomplish it in two separate acts' (GA 4). And then again: 'There are two things which are incompatible with one another: productive activity and the simultaneous contemplation of it' (ibid.). In ego-consciousness on this side of the threshold this is indeed absolutely impossible. But at the moment when ego-consciousness enters the spiritual world in the manner described, it is no longer a 'simultaneous contemplation' that is associated with the 'productive activity' of thinking but, rather, an intuitive living and weaving within it. Furthermore, this merging of the active engendering of thinking and the simultaneous observation of it is the only solid starting point in the spiritual world for the modern clairvoyance which must be developed amongst mankind from our time onwards in accordance with spiritual science.[4] And this clairvoyance, which springs from the source of a transformed thinking, has the task of becoming a new organ for the perceiving of the etheric Christ. For 'in the present age of intellectuality He can appear only in etheric form. Spiritual science wishes to prepare human beings for this' (GA 130, 18 November 1911).

This is an indication of what is the only sure path of awakening man in our time to his higher ego; for he arrives at this in the right way only if, as the starting point of his path, he can maintain the consciousness of his earthly ego within the spiritualized intellectuality.

This awakening in the higher ego has a comparable relationship to the second supersensible revelation of Christ as has the earthly ego living in transformed thinking to Christ's appearance in the etheric. The first revelation, which has begun in the twentieth century and will last for approximately 3000 years, takes place on the astral plane; whereas the second is enacted in Lower Devachan, where the essential nature of the higher ego likewise belongs. In the still more distant future a yet higher Christ revelation will ensue: His appearance in His Ego Being in Higher Devachan.

If one considers that in the book already referred to, *The Threshold of the Spiritual World*, the environment of the 'other self' (higher ego) is the *spiritual* world and of the true ego the *super-spiritual* world, which Rudolf Steiner elsewhere calls Lower and Higher Devachan,[5] the relationship of the two future revelations of Christ to man's higher and true ego emerges, just as His present revelation is connected with the spiritualizing of the earthly ego.

Rudolf Steiner also summarizes all three forms of the supersensible revelation of Christ in the following way: 'So we see how the Christ, who descended to the Earth in a physical, earthly human vessel, gradually evolves as an etheric, an astral and an ego Christ in order as ego Christ to become the Spirit of the Earth, who then rises to ever higher stages with all human beings' (GA 130, 21 September 1911). The still higher stages of His revelation will take place in the sixth great period of human evolution, which will come after the seventh cultural epoch and the War of All against All. One can also say: Just as the second revelation will accompany the uniting of the Earth with the Moon,[6] so will the third revelation of Christ prepare its union with the Sun.

We find a further aspect of this theme in the lecture of 18 November 1911 (GA 130). Here Rudolf Steiner describes the last three post-Atlantean cultural epochs from the standpoint of the three supersensible revelations of Christ and characterizes the present fifth cultural epoch as the age of intellectuality, the sixth as the age of spiritual feelings and emotions and the seventh as the moral age.[7] At the same time he connects the spiritual impulses active in these epochs—intellectual, feeling-oriented and moral will impulses—respectively with those regions of the spiritual world whence the three ascending Christ revelations will take place. In other lectures Rudolf Steiner mentions further qualities of Christ's future revelations: 'Then will come an age when the Christ will manifest Himself in a still higher way: in an astral form in the lower world of Devachan. And the final age, that of moral impulses [the seventh cultural epoch], will be one when the human beings who have passed through the other stages will behold the Christ in His glory, as the form of the greatest "Ego", as the spiritualized Ego Self, as the great Teacher of human evolution in Higher Devachan.' (GA 130, 4 November 1911.) With the support of this third revelation of Christ, the people of this time will be able out of their Christ-imbued ego to withstand the increasing power of evil which will be called forth by the Earth's receiving of the Moon. An ego which has been strengthened in this way will then be able to work in a transforming way into earthly matter. It will also be the time when, after the War of All against All, the whole of earthly life will be imbued with the new sacramentalism which has its origin in the spiritual communion with Christ as the World Ego; and it will be the time when the true Manichaean Mysteries come fully to revelation amongst mankind and will arrive at their highest blossoming.[8]

In another context Rudolf Steiner speaks further about the second supersensible revelation: 'Christ will then [in the sixth cultural epoch] appear in a light-filled form in the world of Lower Devachan to a number of human beings, revealing Himself as sounding Word; and from His astral body of light He will fill their receptive souls with the Word that has been working in astral form from the earliest beginnings, as was set down by John in the opening words of his Gospel. In the age of morality a number of human beings will perceive the Christ revealing Himself from Higher Devachan in His *true Ego* that surpasses all human egos in its inconceivable sublimity, and with such splendour that it can bestow on man the highest possible moral impulses.' (GA 130, 18 November 1911.) For as the creative Word, the power of Christ extends to the world of the fixed stars around our solar system. However, as the ego it reaches still further to those spheres which lie beyond the created cosmos and with which the Ego of Christ has been connected from earliest times. Man's third—true—ego also derives from there,[9] which is why in the description of the third revelation the designation 'true ego' occurs; for the true Ego of Christ is the highest archetype and the source of man's true ego, whence his likeness to God is derived.

It is clear from what has been said that man's ego-development—the essential purpose of the Earth—and the ever-ascending revelations of Christ are inseparably connected with one another. Taking this up into one's ego-consciousness and cultivating it further in one's soul is already the beginning of the path which can lead individual human beings to Christ today.

Rudolf Steiner's words indicating that with the Mystery of Golgotha a new possibility was created of taking one's ego-consciousness and, hence, one's earthly ego into the spiritual world have already been cited. If at this point, however, one would ask which earthly human being has been inherently capable of fully exemplifying this in his life, one again finds oneself approaching the individuality of Jesus of Nazareth.

Thus Rudolf Steiner repeatedly emphasizes that Jesus was no initiate but merely a human being and, hence, at the Baptism in the Jordan stood there as a representative of all humanity. 'The Christ bearer was truly man—not an adept' (GA 131, 7 October 1911).[10] As such he possessed above all the ego-consciousness as manifested through the earthly ego. He was then able to carry this through the Mystery of Golgotha and was the first to take it with him into the spiritual world. Thus he stands before us as a model of this process and also as the great helper in the task which in our time is gradually becoming that of mankind as a whole, that of raising ego-consciousness aloft into the spiritual world on the path of spiritual science.

The threefold relationship of the human ego to the spiritual world which has been described also encompasses its relation to the three beings mentioned in the first chapter, who have a particular part to play in Christ's present appearance in the etheric. Just as the entelechy of Jesus stands for the primordial mystery of the earthly ego, so is it the being of Vidar—in so far as this path after the crossing of the threshold is enabled to continue in the direction of the higher ego—who will help man further on his way. For as the conqueror of the Fenris Wolf, who represents the atavistic forces of the old clairvoyance, Vidar is at the same time man's representative and helper on the path to the higher clairvoyance out of which true spiritual research becomes possible and, hence, the further development of modern, spiritual science. Rudolf Steiner gives an indication on these lines: 'Those who are called upon to interpret from the signs of the time what is to come are aware that the new spiritual research will re-establish the power of Vidar, who will banish from people's minds the confusing influences of the relics of the old, chaotic clairvoyance and will awaken in the human heart, in the human soul the new clairvoyance that is gradually unfolding' (GA 121, 17 June 1910).

And if a person has advanced on the path of modern initiation to the sphere of the true ego, Michael can increasingly become his guide;[11] for as the Sun countenance of Christ and His present emissary amongst mankind,[12] Michael is in our time the great guardian of the new mysteries, at whose centre stands the mystery of Christ and, hence, of man's true ego.

All three beings, the Angel-like being of Jesus of Nazareth,[13] the Archangel Vidar and the Time Spirit Michael, are connected in the manner described with the destiny of the threefold ego in the age of the etheric Christ, whom they serve, together also with those human beings who wish to take their ego-development in hand.[14]

*

From what has been explained in this chapter it remains to ask in what way it was possible for earthly ego-consciousness to be so transformed through Christ's incarnation on the Earth that it can thereafter be taken with one into the spiritual world. The answer emerges from what follows.

The mystery of the threefold ego is revealed with particular clarity in the events of the Turning Point of Time, if these are viewed in the light of what Rudolf Steiner imparted concerning the 'Fifth Gospel'. Thus in the being of Jesus of Nazareth (the Luke Jesus) one can recognize a human being who developed earthly ego-consciousness in an archetypal way— primarily because his incarnation at the Turning Point of Time was his first and only appearance on the Earth, when he took hold of and fully developed an earthly consciousness for the first time. Hence Jesus of Nazareth was able to stand at the Jordan before John the Baptist as the purest representative of earthly humanity, not as an initiate or adept but simply as a human being.

In order to be able to receive the Christ into himself, Jesus of Nazareth had to be prepared for this by one of the highest initiates of the Earth (the individuality of Zarathustra), who lived in him for 18 years and prepared him for his actual task out of the forces of his higher ego: 'To be able to receive the Christ, this bodily nature [of Jesus] had to be prepared, expanded, through the individuality of Zarathustra' (GA 131, 12 October 1911). Thus we find 'the bodily nature [of Jesus] so prepared through the presence of Zarathustra that it could receive the Christ Individuality' (ibid.). In the lectures on the Fifth Gospel Rudolf Steiner says on several occasions that it was above all *the ego* of Zarathustra that had taken hold of Jesus of Nazareth and was active in him for 18 years. However, since this involved a purely spiritual process, only the higher ego of an advanced initiate could bring something of this nature about.

Rudolf Steiner emphasizes that the transition made by the Zarathustra individuality from the Salomonic to the Nathan Jesus boy—which took place around his twelfth year—specifically had to do with the ego of Zarathustra, which had reached so high a stage in its development as to render this possible. It was the higher ego of this individuality that was involved here, which thereupon exerted a preparatory influence in the sheaths of Jesus of Nazareth.

Then Zarathustra made the highest sacrifice. Immediately before the Baptism in the Jordan he left the three sheaths of Jesus of Nazareth, so that the cosmic Christ Being could occupy them. This Being was then active in Jesus for three years with the power and out of the impulse of the true ego, for which Christ is the highest archetype in the spiritual world.

Thus for the first time in the evolution of humanity the power of the true Ego of Christ in Jesus of Nazareth permeated the earthly ego of a human being. In this way the human earthly ego was raised from the stage of appearance to that of being. Since this time every human being has inherently possessed the faculty of fully taking his earthly ego with him into the spiritual world, in order there on the path of modern initiation to unite with the higher and then with the true ego and thereby attain to the highest experience of Christ.

★

The three steps in the evolution of man's ego-organization that have been described here also include a further aspect which should not go without mention. In the first chapter of the book *The Spiritual Guidance of Man and Humanity* (GA 15) Rudolf Steiner indicates how in the first three years of a child's life, that is, before the initial emergence of its ego-consciousness, the forces of the Christ work directly upon the child. They engender three faculties, which must precede the birth of the earthly ego: standing upright (walking), speaking and thinking. These three faculties are engendered by Christ out of the true ego, which—albeit unconsciously—belongs to the child. In standing upright and walking this happens directly out of the true ego, in learning to speak it comes about through the mediation of the higher ego and in thinking there is already the unconscious support of the earthly ego-consciousness that is being formed, which will forthwith be manifested in and through thinking.

If a person—in our time it is only possible for an initiate—were able to take hold of these three faculties in full consciousness, he would enter into a direct connection with the true ego, his higher ego and those forces that lie spiritually at the foundation of his earthly ego. That the three egos of man are indeed connected with the faculties of walking, speaking and thinking underlies the circumstance that they arise in the child, because the beings of the Third Hierarchy make them available to it out of the respective regions of the spiritual world.

Thus the Archai bring to man the predisposition to walk upright out of Higher Devachan (super-spiritual world), to which the first manifestation of man's true ego also belongs.[15] The Archangeloi similarly make available the faculty of speaking out of Lower Devachan (spiritual world), which Rudolf Steiner from a cosmological standpoint brings into connection with the sphere of the Sun. Finally the Angels continue this activity within man and, as the foundation and maternal ground for the subsequent awakening of the earthly ego, implant within him the faculty of thinking, which is manifested in a strong ego-consciousness; for 'by learning to think' the child begins 'to work its way through to the ego' (GA 152, 7 March 1914).[16]

In the lecture-cycle *Man's Being, His Destiny and World Evolution* Rudolf Steiner summarizes this process: 'What we are given by anthroposophy shows us how the divine-spiritual lives everywhere in life's individual phenomena. We look at the way in which the child passes from the clumsy stage of crawling to that of walking. Looking with admiration and reverence at this magnificent world phenomenon, we see in it the work of the *Archai*, who are active when the experiences that we undergo between death and a new birth are transformed into their earthly counterpart. Then we follow the process whereby the child brings forth speech out of its inner self, we follow the activity of the *Archangels*; and, when the child begins to think, the activity of the *Angels*.' (GA 226, 18 May 1923.) Only once man has taken hold of uprightness, speaking and thinking with the help of the supersensible forces of the Third Hierarchy can his ego-consciousness be fully kindled on this foundation as a direct manifestation of the awakened earthly ego. That he can inherently reach this decisive stage of human nature, however, he is indebted to the Christ event at the Turning Point of Time, the Mystery of Golgotha.

For the shining forth of the earthly ego is a direct consequence of the Christ event: 'The Mystery of Golgotha has inaugurated the unfolding of a strong ego-consciousness for earthly humanity. This ego-consciousness has gradually come to pervade human culture since the Mystery of Golgotha, but especially from the first third of the fifteenth century [the beginning of the consciousness-soul epoch]. The effect of this strong ego-consciousness is that man places himself as a free, fully conscious being in the world of the senses' (GA 226, 18 May 1923).

It follows from this, however, that when man receives the Christ impulse in freedom into his earthly ego and imbues his ego-consciousness with it through the further development of thinking, he can in the sense of modern initiation find the path up to his higher and subsequently to his true ego, but in such a way that he fully preserves the integrity of his earthly ego.

The full consciousness of the earthly ego also plays a decisive role in preparing for a true experience of the etheric Second Coming. Thus through the study of spiritual science and above all its Christology, the union of the two streams of man's etherized blood—which leads to a perception of the etheric Christ—is achieved.[17] This refers pre-eminently to study, which Rudolf Steiner defines in the book *Occult Science* as the first stage of modern initiation: 'The study of spiritual science, where one avails oneself of the power of judgement which one has gained in the physical world of the senses' (GA 13). This power of judgement is achieved in the physical world of the senses wholly through the active input of the earthly ego. The same also applies to Christ's appearance as the Lord of Karma.

If a person prepares himself for this encounter with the Lord of Karma already on Earth—and this can happen in our time only through spiritual science—but not out of his ego-consciousness, such an encounter can only call forth terror and horror within him. He will not be able to understand it and will experience it simply as a cruel punishment. Rudolf Steiner says in this regard: 'The beholding of the Christ event does not depend on whether we are incarnated in a physical body [for the Christ event can also be experienced in the spiritual world after a person's death], but the *preparation* for it does. Just as it was necessary for the first Christ event to take place on the physical plane in order that man's redemption could be accomplished, so must the preparation be made here in the physical world to look with full understanding, with full illumination, upon the Christ event of the twentieth century. For a person who looks upon it unprepared, when his powers have been awakened, will not be able to understand it. The Lord of Karma will then appear to him as a terrible punishment.' (GA 131, 14 Ocxtober 1911.) And then Rudolf Steiner adds these decisive words: 'The spreading of the anthroposophical world-conception is taking place in our time so that people can be prepared on the physical plane or on higher planes' (ibid.). This preparation likewise happens out of the pure force of the earthly ego, so that a person can fully retain his freedom in encountering the Lord of Karma.

As has been pointed out earlier (see chapter 2), the necessary connection of earthly ego-consciousness with the present Christ event also arises through spiritual science or anthroposophy, if it is regarded as the spiritual language in which human beings in our time are able to pose the most important questions to the etheric Christ. Rudolf Steiner says about this: 'So let us seek to acquire a relationship to spiritual science not merely as a teaching but as a language and wait until we find the questions in this language that we may address to Christ. He will answer, yes, He *will* answer!' (GA 175, 6 February 1917, italics Rudolf Steiner.)

The three ways of experiencing Christ in the present which have been briefly described here can be summarized as follows:

human beings will perceive Him as an etheric manifestation (Imagination);

they will receive from Him an answer to the questions they pose to
Him in the language of spiritual science (Inspiration);
and experience Him as the Lord of Karma (Intuition).

In the encounter with Christ as the Lord of Karma on the intuitional
plane, the same forces are active which also bring about an upright posture
in the little child through the mediation of the Archai. In the apprehending of Christ's answers to the questions posed on the part of spiritual
science, the Archangeloi are working on the plane of Inspiration. And as
Christ is beheld in His etheric form the Angels are working on the
imaginative plane, helping man to transform his thinking into the faculty
of the new clairvoyance,[18] so that the light springing from this can radiate
together with the light of Christ in the spiritual world bordering upon the
Earth.

In all three experiences which can be characterized as our relationship
to Christ today, ego-consciousness forms the starting point and the
foundation, which springs from the earthly ego and—through working
with spiritual science (the study of anthroposophy)—prepares man so that
subsequently he can consciously and freely encounter the etheric Christ in
the spiritual world. For only through an inner relationship with this most
important event of our time can man indeed have a part in 'recognizing
and realizing the intentions of the *living Christ*, wherein lies the 'essential
meaning of the Earth'.[19]

4. Memory and Conscience in the Light of the Second Coming

One of the last letters that Rudolf Steiner wrote at the end of his life in connection with the 'Leading Thoughts' for the members of the Anthroposophical Society in February 1925 bears the title 'Memory and Conscience' (GA 26). In it, he shows how through these two soul faculties man is connected with the spiritual world as though from two sides also during his waking life.

With memory the forces of the physical-etheric starry cosmos radiate into the bodily organization through the mediation of the head and thought system; and in the voice of conscience the limb and will system enables the consequences of its intercourse with divine-spiritual beings during sleep to be revealed. In the middle, rhythmic system both of man's relationships to the divine-spiritual world are brought into a mutual interconnection. Through the rhythmic activity of the heart and lungs the memory-forces are brought into the will sphere and the power of conscience into the life of ideas. (See GA 26, Leading Thought 176.) Despite this balancing activity of the middle system, people are generally organized more in one or the other direction.

In the one group the forces of memory predominate. If such people are artistically inclined or creatively gifted in some way, forces of fantasy are aroused to a significant degree by the spirituality living in memory. In such an 'activity of fancy, the thinking system reaches towards the will organization' (ibid.). These people are then inclined to experience 'the content of their souls as dreams in a waking state'. Through this they naturally possess an inclination towards perceiving imaginations.[1]

With the other group, who are in a certain respect the complete opposite of the first, the guiding forces of the soul derive from the region of the will. If such people are creative and artistically inclined, they seek in the first instance to develop their imaginative content from the realm of the will. With them 'the inner love for the ideal world-view' plays a significant role. They are quite particularly receptive to the voice of conscience and have a natural inclination towards Inspiration.

Ahriman and Lucifer take account of these two types of people in their intentions for the world. The ahrimanic power endeavours to separate those souls who base their inner activity more on the spirituality of memory-forces from the past, in order to guide them into the direction of development that it has planned. If this were to happen, a further moral development for these souls would become possible only with difficulty. On the other hand, the luciferic power tries to bind those people who belong to the other group, and are inclined to allow their lives to be influenced by their conscience, wholly to the past. These people are indeed able to develop into moral beings, but all the morality that they bear comes to be of an automatic nature and is strongly oriented around outward norms, rules and precepts.

As particular representatives of these two groups, in whom of course the most diverse nuances of soul are to be found, Rudolf Steiner refers to the inner orientation of Goethe and Schiller, in whom the finest qualities of the respective groups were manifested, which is why they complemented one another in so wonderful a way after they had formed a friendship with one another. Thus Schiller was able to interpret Goethe's 'poetic dreams', making it possible for him to understand them ever more consciously and use them in his literary work. It also helped him to find the path from Imagination to Inspiration. Goethe, on the other hand, represented to his friend through his whole artistic personality the picture of an ideal human being, which Schiller already bore in himself as an intellectual quality of Inspiration but lacked the corresponding perception for it, that is, the faculty of Imagination. Thus through his acquaintance with Goethe, Schiller was able to advance from his original predisposition towards intellectual Inspiration to the development of true Imagination in his artistic creativity.[2]

Thus in Goethe and Schiller the capacity of experiencing the two principal aspects of the etheric Second Coming was as it were prophetically anticipated. And although in their time the possibility of beholding Christ in the etheric was not as yet available to them, one can regard their soul-spiritual organization as models for what must be inwardly developed by people today in order to be abreast of the requirements of our time with respect to the experience of the etheric Christ. What is actually meant by this will become clear from what follows.

It is significant that Rudolf Steiner explicitly mentions the two human faculties referred to above in connection with the influence of the etheric Christ. For in our time memory and conscience must gradually pass through a kind of metamorphosis and further development in order to become new organs for the perception of the etheric Second Coming.

Thus Rudolf Steiner describes how one of the essential changes that will gradually be seen in the human organization from our time onwards in connection with the etheric Second Coming consists in Christ's involvement with the human faculty of memory, which will bring about its total transformation. 'The new Christ event, which is now approaching, not physically but etherically, is connected with the first kindling of the faculty of memory that is imbued by Christ, where Christ approaches man as an angelic being. We must prepare ourselves for this.' (GA 152, 7 March 1914.)

This transformation of the faculty of memory will occupy a long time in human history and extend over the rest of the fifth and also over the whole of the sixth and seventh cultural epochs of the Earth, until the beginning of the sixth great period of the Earth, when the Christ power will be constantly present in the memory of human beings. 'And a time will arrive for humanity which will only come to fulfilment in the sixth greater period of human evolution (but is now being prepared) when people will look upon what they have experienced, which lives in them as memory, and will be able to see that Christ lives with them in the power of memory. Christ will be able to speak through every memory-picture.' (Ibid.)

This process is inwardly connected with an ever stronger experience on the part of human individuals of the familiar words of the Apostle Paul: 'It is no longer I who live, but Christ who lives in me' (Galatians 2:20) or, in Rudolf Steiner's summary translation, 'Not I, but Christ in me.' 'The path that has been laid down for human beings to make more and more true the words, "Not I, but Christ in me", will be made smooth through Christ's gradually becoming involved with the power of memory' (ibid.). In this way the Christ impulse will enter into a completely new relationship with man's earthly ego; for the effectiveness of the ego is unfolded in earthly circumstances only on the foundation of the faculty of memory.[3] However, man does not take this with him into the spiritual world—and, hence, also not his earthly ego-consciousness. But if the power of Christ unites with memory and awakens it out of its primordial shadowy existence through its being transformed by man into a true imaginative life, this can become possible for him.

Thus man finds Christ in a completely new way in his earthly consciousness, that is, as a personal inner experience whereby (as was already described in chapter 3) he is increasingly able to take his earthly ego-consciousness into the spiritual world, in order there to attain to true immortality.

Through this intervention of the power of Christ in the capacity of memory, the whole history of mankind will come to be experienced in two parts: that time when Christ was only to be found outside the Earth and guided earthly evolution from the Sun; and from the moment when Christ fully and wholly united Himself with the evolution of mankind through the Mystery of Golgotha, in order to continue working within human history. This will in future times become an ever more profound personal experience for human beings. The whole history of the world will, as a result, resurrect in the light of the memory that has been enlivened by Christ as something living. And from its midst the Christ event of the Turning Point of Time will shine forth towards man as the fulcrum of the whole evolution of the world (see ibid.).

In the same lecture Rudolf Steiner refers to the counter-picture of this future, which will come about if mankind does not succeed in taking the etheric Christ into its faculty of memory. In such a case it will in time get into an ever greater state of disorder and, even, rush headlong into a kind of chaos; for 'our capacity for remembering can only develop properly if the Christ impulse is viewed in the right way' (ibid.). And as the faculty of memory descends into chaos, man's ego-consciousness, the most important achievement of the whole of earthly evolution, will increasingly enter into a state of complete insanity. During the next 3000 years of the etheric Second Coming of Christ, the destiny of human memory and, hence, of the earthly ego for the rest of earthly evolution will be resolved on this basis. Thus everything depends on which evolutionary path human beings freely decide to follow.

In order that a right decision regarding this question can be arrived at, Rudolf Steiner gave a meditation to guide us on our path which is uniquely able to facilitate an encounter with the etheric Christ through the conscious transformation of the inner powers of memory:

> In the beginning is memory,
> And memory lives on,
> And divine is memory,
> And memory is life,
> And this life is the human 'I',
> Which flows in man himself.
> Not he alone, but Christ in him.
> When he remembers divine life
> Christ is in his remembering,
> And as the radiant life of memory
> Will Christ shine
> In every immediately present darkness.[4]

*

The etheric Second Coming will also have a decisive influence on the faculty of conscience. Thus this mysterious voice in the human soul will gradually—though beginning already in our time—experience a significant change. From its originally still somewhat abstract form of influence as a more or less undefined voice in the deeper layers of the soul, conscience will develop into an organ of new karmic vision. This comes about as follows. After carrying out a deed a person will feel the inclination to have an inner debate with himself and reflect about the accomplished action. In the course of this a picture—an imagination—will, albeit at first only dimly, arise as a kind of dream in the soul. If, with the preparation that anthroposophy can give, he is able to deepen this imagination meditatively, its real significance will light up in his mind. It will show him what he must do in the future in order to compensate for the deed that was previously accomplished increasingly in accordance with the cosmic order as a whole. Thus a person who has understood the significance of such an imagination will say to himself: 'Now I have done this, and I am being shown what I shall have to do by way of compensation and what I shall lack in perfection until the compensation has been made' (GA 116, 8 May 1910). In this way he will 'see in pictures ... the effect of his deeds for the future' (ibid.). That he can advance to this higher soul-faculty will be the consequence of the fact that, as preparation for this higher stage through many incarnations, he has lived under the influence of the voice of conscience.

The decisive aspect of this situation, however, will be that people come to be able to recognize the true significance of this picture so as then *freely* to follow the path of implementing the compensatory act indicated to them. This resolve, together with a right understanding of the situation in its entirety, will become possible only if they have previously found a conscious relationship to Christ; for behind this whole process of transformation of human conscience stands Christ's present activity as the Lord of Karma. And to the extent that man increasingly learns also to act out of his 'intuitive conscience', he will arrive at a direct perception of Christ as the Lord of Karma. For this, however, the corresponding preparation out of anthroposophy is necessary. Otherwise a person who has gradually succeeded in beholding Christ as the Lord of Karma will not derive from this a mighty impulse for further development but 'the Lord of Karma will then appear to him as a terrible punishment' (GA 131, 14 October 1911).

In this way man will gradually make his way into the spiritual sphere whence Christ begins to work in our time as the Lord of Karma.[5] What does this office actually consist in? Rudolf Steiner describes it in the following words: 'To ensure that our karmic account will be balanced in the future—that is, made part of the cosmic order with respect to that future time when we have found our way to Christ—in such a way that our karmic compensation will bring the greatest possible benefit for humanity for the rest of earthly evolution, this will be the concern of Him who from our time onwards is becoming the Lord of Karma, it will be the concern of Christ. However, Christ's assuming of the office of judging human deeds is associated with His direct intervention in human destiny.' (GA 130, 2 December 1911.)

What is meant here is that the law of karma as the principle of cosmic justice continues to be upheld.[6] However, the paths to its fulfilment take increasingly manifold forms. The task of Christ will be to balance out deeds that have been accomplished in such a way that the general progress and spiritual well-being of mankind will be immeasurably enhanced. And in the imaginations referred to earlier Christ will place the possible compensatory states before the inner eye of human beings such that they can in working on their personal karma increasingly become servants and spiritual helpers in the general advancement of mankind. In this way the whole evolution of mankind on Earth will be accelerated to a remarkable degree in the direction of the good. 'This will give a powerful stimulus to human morality, and this stimulus will signify something quite different from the voice of conscience, which has been a preparation for it' (GA 131, 14 October 1911). In the fourth part of the Foundation Stone Meditation this state of affairs is characterized in the following words:

O Light Divine,
O Sun of Christ,
Warm Thou
Our Hearts,
Enlighten Thou
Our Heads,
That good may become ...'

(GA 260, 25 December 1923)

So out of the conscious permeation of human hearts and heads with the power of the Sun of Christ the goodness in the world will be enormously strengthened. Rudolf Steiner points in the same direction with the following sentence from the ninth chapter of his *Philosophy of Freedom*, even though the name of Christ is not mentioned here: 'I do not work out mentally whether my action is good or bad; I carry it out because I *love* it. My action will be "good" if my intuition, steeped in love, finds its right place within the intuitively experienceable world continuum; it will be "bad" if this is not the case.' (GA 4, italics Rudolf Steiner.) But from the spiritual point of view the greatest 'world continuum' is the one in which the Mystery of Golgotha and its spiritual consequences stand and where in our time the appearance of Christ as the Lord of Karma occupies a place of particular importance.[7] Hence, the relationship to the Lord of Karma is an integral part of 'the intuitively experienceable world continuum' and, in its further development, leads to a collaboration with Him.

Whether human beings will respond to the imaginative pictures which Christ shows them in the manner described and which establish a connection with ever wider aspects of the world order is henceforth in their own hands. That is why this perspective of the future does not by any means signify a restriction of human freedom but merely an extending of man's knowledge and the growth of his responsibility in the realm of karma. In this way man will in turn become Christ's conscious collaborator in this field.

★

Summing up what has been presented here one can say that the supersensible Christ event is being prepared and brought about from our time onwards from two sides: as Christ's appearance in the etheric body and as His appearance as the Lord of Karma. Similarly in man himself this path to the etheric Christ can be characterized by two different aspects: the transforming of his memory and its permeation by Christ;[8] and the new kind of conscience, which gradually becomes ever more intuitive or visionary, in the realm of karma.

If one also adds that a development in both these directions—the transformation of memory and conscience—can be strengthened by the study of anthroposophy and regular meditative work, a new light is shed on the three principal exercises of the Foundation Stone Meditation. In the sense of its fourth part the light of the 'Sun of Christ' can illumine the realm of memory from a Christian standpoint and warm the realm of visionary conscience, which comes to manifestation in man's readiness also to follow the imaginative premonition of his compensatory deeds. In this way the conscious relationship to Christ, which can already be achieved through the study of anthroposophy ('Practise spirit-mindfulness'), leads on the one hand to His influence on the human memory ('Practise spirit-remembering') and on the other to the active participation of Christ in the visionary conscience ('Practise spirit-vision').

As indicated in the letter referred to at the outset on 'Memory and Conscience', the path of imbuing the human memory with Christ also signifies a striving for a new and conscious connection with the etheric cosmos whence Christ appears in His etheric manifestation. And the transformation of conscience through Christ as the Lord of Karma will bring man into a new relationship with the spiritual world, that is, with those hierarchic beings who are responsible for the right moulding of human karma and who previously, when man was not yet ripe for conscious collaboration in this domain, led his karma to fulfilment through the voice of conscience.

The developments which have been sketched in connection with the etheric Second Coming will also have a considerable influence on social life; for the transformation of memory will bring it about that a human individual experiences the whole history of humanity far stronger than before and as belonging to his own, more extensive biography, which stands in a direct relationship to his former, present and future earthly deeds, for which he bears personal responsibility at every moment of his life. At the same time the further training of conscience through the growing awareness of karma will unite him more and more with mankind. And in the light of Christ as the Lord of Karma he will increasingly be able to fashion and lead his life in the context of humanity as a whole. In this way the foundation for the brotherly union of all human beings is laid which, through the unfolding of the forces of wonder, love *and conscience*, then becomes the great organism in which Christ can participate as a new group soul, or as the true Ego.[9] 'Human beings will then in the course of earthly evolution lay the foundations for a great community which can be fully pervaded, fully imbued by the Christ impulse' (GA 155, 30 May 1912).

However, both adversarial powers are working against this evolutionary path. As we have already seen, Rudolf Steiner characterizes their influence in the letter referred to by saying that Ahriman would seek to cut human beings off from memory, above all from their memory of the Mystery of Golgotha; and Lucifer wants to bind them to their old karma in such a way that a transformation in the sense of visionary conscience does not become possible, that people are unable to recognize the karmic imaginations that have been inspired and guided by Christ as belonging to themselves and do not want to respond to them in their deeds.

With this is connected a quite particular aspect of the sculptural Group, where Christ as the Representative of Humanity defeats and overcomes both kinds of adversary by establishing a balance between them. Through this, access to Christ's deed on Golgotha is kept constantly open, while on the other hand the new collaboration with Him in the realm of karma is made possible. Thus in this unique work of art the twofold mystery of the etheric Second Coming is brought to expression.

How was Rudolf Steiner himself able to arrive at this aspect of his sculpture, that is, discover this twofold mystery of the etheric Second

Coming? This was only possible because he had himself fully imbued his memory and his conscience with the Christ impulse and was therefore able out of his Christ-imbued memory to experience the Mystery of Golgotha as the centre of the whole of world evolution and, hence, also portray this in his work of art. And out of his Christ-imbued conscience he could be the first to proclaim Christ's new office as the Lord of Karma and, by directly collaborating with Him in this domain, was enabled to entrust to human beings the mighty fruits of his karma research, which found their culmination in his revelation of the karma of anthroposophists and of that of the General Anthroposophical Society founded at Christmas 1923. With this, Rudolf Steiner laid the foundation on which all people of good will who truly take the karma lectures into their hearts and seek to embrace them with their souls, can, as a new karmic community on the Earth, take the first steps towards collaborating with Christ as the Lord of Karma.

5. The Etheric Christ and the Michael Spirit Who Serves Him

'I have frequently emphasized in
various lecture cycles that in
November 1879 that spiritual being
whom we call the Archangel Michael
has reached a particular stage of
development. Michael became, so to
speak, the ruling spirit. This ruling
spirit is now preparing the event
which in the first of my mystery plays
is intimated as being the appearance
of the etheric Christ over the Earth.'

Rudolf Steiner[1]

Rudolf Steiner's entire activity—from his early philosophical work to his very last letters, which form a kind of culmination and the conclusion of his earthly activity as a Christian initiate and spiritual teacher—stands under the sign of the Michael mystery, which is inseparably connected with man's freedom and his new relationship to Christ.

Rudolf Steiner based the nature of freedom in his *Philosophy of Freedom* on 'purely human faculties of cognition'. At the end of his life he established 'the cosmic nature of *freedom*' in the light of the Michael mystery.[2] From this Michaelic investigation of the nature of human freedom the modern path to Christ also becomes discernible; for only in him and with him do people in our time find a true foundation for their freedom in the epoch of the consciousness soul.

It is Michael himself who reveals the Mystery of Golgotha today as the source of human freedom, on whose foundation alone true love can unfold. 'That we can be free beings we owe to a divine deed of love. So as human individuals we may feel ourselves to be free beings, but we should never forget that we owe this freedom to a deed of divine love ... People would not be able to take hold of the idea of freedom without the thought of redemption through Christ. Only then is the notion of freedom justified. If we want to be free, we must make the offering of thanks to Christ for our freedom!' (GA 131, 14 October 1911).

In the light of the Michael mystery one can find the esoteric foundation of the words just quoted in the following description by Rudolf Steiner:

'Michael can give us new spiritual light, which we may regard as a transformation of the light given through him at the time of the Mystery of Golgotha, *and the people of our time may receive this light*' (GA 152, 2 May 1913).[3] Receiving this light of Michael means in our time that we 'understand the new truth of the Mystery of Golgotha' (ibid.), that is, approach the Mystery of Golgotha at the Turning Point of Time in the spirit of its repetition in the spiritual world bordering upon the Earth in our time. (See chapter 7.)

★

In the letters about the Michael mystery Rudolf Steiner characterizes the being of Michael by saying that he has participated in the evolution of mankind from the beginning. 'The spiritual being who has from the beginning directed his gaze towards mankind is Michael. He so orders the activities of the Gods that in one part of the cosmos mankind may exist.'[4]

He is also the spirit who, in order to create the *conditions* for the subsequent development of human freedom, cast the luciferic spirits down from the higher spiritual spheres into the human domain in Lemurian times, which in the Bible is described as the Fall of Man. Rudolf Steiner formulates this as follows: ' "And he cast his opposing spirits down upon the Earth", that is, through this casting down of the luciferic spirits who oppose Michael man was imbued with his power of reason, with what springs from the human head' (GA 194, 22 November 1919).

Thus it is obvious that an aspect of Michael's task in participating in the Fall of Man—which happened at the behest of still higher spirits—was to protect a part of the being of Adam, the 'sister soul' of the first human being already referred to, from succumbing to the luciferic spirits.[5] Since then he has been this being's guardian in the higher worlds and, since then, the guardian of man's heavenly likeness. That this is indeed the case is apparent from certain variants of the so-called 'Golden Legend', according to which Michael was called upon to guard the Tree of Life, or the two intertwined trees (of knowledge and of life), from the assault of the so-called adversarial powers and from being seized hold of by 'fallen' human beings.

In the first chapter there was a reference to Michael's direct participation in the third preliminary stage of the Mystery of Golgotha, whence also derives his involvement with the first two stages, because he is active wherever the battle in the name of Christ against the adversarial powers is being waged. He is always the one who keeps the dragon beneath his feet.

It was from the Sun that Michael experienced the Mystery of Golgotha, through which the spiritual centre of our cosmic system was transferred from the Sun, that is, from that realm which he himself serves, to the Earth. The path of Christ from the Sun to the realm of human beings was soon also followed by the cosmic intelligence or intellectuality, which Michael had ruled over from the earliest beginnings. Its stream reached the Earth in the eighth/ninth centuries. People experience it by increasingly feeling themselves inwardly as the creators of their own thoughts. In the course of this the basis for freedom was implanted in the souls of human beings.

With the beginning of the consciousness-soul epoch (1413) this new faculty of individual thought formation entered more into people's possession, so that they will gradually reach the sphere of freedom. From this the danger also arises that the intelligence now living within them, which formerly belonged to Michael, is overwhelmed by the ahrimanic spirits. The whole development of modern science shows that this happened in the ensuing centuries. This did indeed originate in the Christian evolution of humanity (see GA 148, 1 October 1913), but its increasingly materialistic orientation is indicative of the ever stronger preponderance of ahrimanic powers. Thus the fate of the ahrimanic intelligence lies to a certain extent as never before in the hands of human beings. The battle in this domain for the Michaelic impulse on the Earth is developing today with a particular intensity. With this comes the all-determining question: will the true science of the spirit gradually pervade and ultimately transform earthly civilization in accordance with Michael's rulership alongside natural science in our time, or will the ahrimanic powers finally hold sway over earthly evolution through the further spread of materialism?[6]

Thus in our time man is confronted with the need to decide between Michael and Ahriman for his further development. In order that this decision can be taken amongst mankind in accordance with the good gods who are its guide, Michael first inaugurated his supersensible school in the spiritual world for the time from the fifteenth until the eighteenth century and subsequently also the cosmic cultus, with the object of preparing the souls of human beings in the spiritual world between two incarnations for this battle around his intelligence, which will later be fought out in human hearts. For this battle must to all intents and purposes be won by Michael already during this present rulership over mankind (from 1879 until around 2300). 'This battle, more than any other, is enacted in the human heart ... And in the course of the twentieth century, when the first century after the end of Kali Yuga has elapsed, humanity will either be standing at the grave of all civilization or at the beginning of that age when—in the souls of those people who in their hearts unite intelligence with spirituality—Michael's battle will be fought through to victory' (GA 240, 19 July 1924). And in this decisive battle human hearts must pre-eminently 'become the helpers of Michael in the conquering of the intelligence that has fallen to the Earth' (ibid.).

In order to play his part in this process, Michael left the Sun sphere and gradually came down to the spiritual world bordering upon the Earth. This path corresponded in the development of Michael himself to his ascent from the rank of Archangel to that of Archai; and since 1879 he has been the present Time Spirit of mankind. Rudolf Steiner indicates that Michael pursues this path as a kind of imitation of the cosmic path of the Christ Being: 'The Archangel Michael had to prepare himself to descend to the Earth itself, as it were in emulation of the great process involving Christ Jesus Himself,[7] taking his starting point here upon the Earth and continuing to be active from the Earth's standpoint' (GA 174a, 17 February 1918).

This means that, since the beginning of his present regency, Michael has been increasingly wanting to make his new dwelling in the hearts of human beings, in order from there again to take up the rulership of the intelligence which Ahriman has wrested from them. 'Michael, who has been striving from the Sun for those on Earth who perceive the spiritual in the cosmos, wants in the future to establish his dwelling-place in the hearts and souls of earthly human beings' (GA 240, 21 August 1924). For only if this happens can he indicate to human individuals the path that leads them from Ahriman's kingdom to Christ. 'Michael cannot force human beings to do anything. For it is just through intelligence having come entirely into the sphere of the human individuality that compulsion has ceased. But in the supersensible world immediately bordering upon the visible world, Michael can develop what he wishes to manifest as a majestic, exemplary deed.'[8] What he thus develops in the first instance in the spiritual world is the revelation of the divine, spiritual light of primal beginnings. In this light of the primordial cosmic intelligence, which he brings out of the past into the present and in which there is nothing luciferic,[9] he can show human individuals as a model for their actions 'how *for him* Ahriman will always be the lower spirit under his feet' (ibid., italics Rudolf Steiner).

Those people who open themselves to this new revelation of Michael through spiritual science can experience thereby 'how, *through the picture of Michael* in Ahriman's sphere, man is to be led in freedom away from Ahriman to Christ' (ibid.). This is indicative of the macrocosmic process through which Michael also leads the human souls who belong to him to an experience of the etheric Christ. According to Rudolf Steiner's spiritual research, the beholding of the etheric Christ is connected with the uniting of both streams of etherized blood in the human heart: the human microcosmic stream and the macrocosmic stream of Christ, which since the Mystery of Golgotha can be found in every human individual. (See GA 130, 1 October 1911.) However, this union within man can take place only if his heart has been completely freed from the dragon forces which have crept into it in the course of earthly evolution.[10]

Rudolf Steiner describes how this happens in the lecture of 27 September 1923, where he says that there exists a microcosmic path—within man himself—corresponding to the macrocosmic path indicated from Michael to Christ; for in our time the Michael forces are also at work in a quite particular way within man. They appear today in him in the form of the etheric image of Michael which reflects the cosmic deeds of the Time Spirit in the human etheric body.

This is what Rudolf Steiner means when he reports how in recent centuries of Western evolution human individuals have, as a result of their pre-birth encounter with Michael, been enabled to take a supersensible picture of him into their etheric bodies when incarnating on the Earth. For if Michael were to pervade man's being with his full cosmic power, people could never remain free. Hence for the sake of human freedom Michael sends only his reflection to man's being, which can then be perceived by a clairvoyant in the region of the head or, to be more precise, more in the direction of the rear of the head. And now, with the beginning of the present Michael epoch in 1879, this reflection of Michael in man's etheric body has become so strong that victory over the forces of the dragon can indeed come about in human hearts. 'Then the power of Michael crushing the dragon would become visible in this human head, but extending his influence down to the heart, causing the dragon's blood to flow from man's heart to his limbs' (GA 223, 27 September 1923). And then Rudolf Steiner continues: 'Within man there lives an etheric image of Michael that wages the real battle which enables man gradually to become free in the campaigns of Michael; for it is not Michael who wages the battle but human devotion and the image of Michael which is called forth by it' (ibid.).

With the beginning of the Michael epoch in the last third of the nineteenth century, this 'etheric mirror-image' of Michael within man has become so strong that through 'human devotion' to him the spiritual power residing in him can be taken hold of and used by man in order to free the spiritual heart region from the dragon forces rising up from the lower abdomen. In this way, protection can be given to the inner space where the connection of the etherized stream of human blood with the etherized blood of Christ can come about (this connection was described above on p. 18f.). In our time this leads to the possibility of beholding Christ in His etheric manifestation.

Thus we have this twofold activity of Michael in the service of the etheric Christ. In the macrocosm he battles for the spiritual space in which Christ can appear before human beings in an undistorted imagination. And what is this space? It is the space where the etheric Second Coming is taking place today and which represents a kind of paradise transformed by the Resurrection of Christ. In old oriental traditions this space is called 'Shamballa', where the primal forces of mankind are preserved. It is also the place where after the Fall the new Tree of Paradise which arose out of the intertwining of both trees—of knowledge and of life—is guarded by Michael. (See GA 96, 17 December 1906.)

Rudolf Steiner says of this ancient 'fairy-tale land' of Shamballa in its connection with the Second Coming: 'Thus at the time when people will be least inclined to believe in documents, the new profession of faith in Christ Jesus will arise through our growing into the sphere in which we shall initially encounter Him, through our growing into the mysterious land of Shamballa . . . Among the first things that people will behold when Shamballa becomes visible once more will be Christ in His etheric form' (GA 118, 6 March 1910). Rudolf Steiner describes the reappearing land of Shamballa as a spiritual realm in the Earth's aura which is 'imbued and irradiated with light' and 'abounding in infinite fullness of life' (ibid.). Both its principal qualities—light and life—are indicative of the dual nature of the Tree of Paradise, with the Tree of Knowledge and the Tree of Life. Whence do this light and life enter the land of Shamballa, where the etheric Christ appears today as the bearer of cosmic love?

Michael has in our time decisively exemplified the process of filling the new land of Shamballa with spiritual light. Already in grey antiquity the true initiates of mankind and also the bodhisattvas again and again derived the spiritual forces of their higher knowledge from this land.[11] For it has from the outset had a connection with the cosmic intelligence of the past, with regard to which Michael has the task in our time to make it accessible in a new way to mankind in the context of the union of the two trees. 'Michael can show himself there with an aura of light, with the gesture of a spirit-being, in which all the splendour and glory of the past intelligence of the Gods is revealed. There he can make it apparent that the influence of this intelligence of the past in the present is more true, more beautiful and more virtuous than everything that has to do with the intelligence of the immediate present, which streams to us in deceptive, misleading splendour.'[12]

Moreover, this 'past intelligence of the Gods'—in so far as it is protected by Michael—has nothing luciferic about it: 'The manner in which Michael brings the past into activity in present human life is one which is in accordance with the true spiritual progress of the world and contains nothing luciferic.'[13]

In this way Michael achieves a perfect balance between the luciferic and ahrimanic powers in revealing the light of the intelligence of the Gods and hence, in the sense of Rudolf Steiner's sculptural Group, becomes the present guide to Christ: 'To have this attitude towards the *light of Michael* which is dawning in human history also means to be able to find the right path to Christ' (ibid.).

Michael is able to open up to human individuals this new path to Christ, which emerges from a state of equilibrium between the forces of Ahriman and Lucifer and finds its artistic expression in Rudolf Steiner's sculptural Group, because on two occasions, first over the luciferic and then over the ahrimanic powers, he has already been victorious over them in the evolution of mankind. Thus at the beginning of earthly evolution he cast the hosts of the luciferic spirits from higher spiritual spheres down to the Earth, which led to the so-called Fall of Man, or the endowing of man with an independent power of reason.

In the autumn of 1879, after a decade of incessant spiritual battle in the supersensible worlds, Michael then cast a horde of ahrimanic spirits— referred to by Rudolf Steiner as 'spirits of darkness'—down to the Earth. (See GA 177, 14 October 1917.) By this means the ahrimanic dragon gained direct access to the human etheric body. At the same time, as we have already seen, Michael implanted his likeness in man's etheric body, in order that man can find the inner strength himself to conquer the ahrimanic dragon in his heart. This also corresponds to man's present path to Christ, on which—with Michael's help—man establishes a balance in his own being between the luciferic forces active in his head and the ahrimanic power of the dragon rising up from the region of the will, from his limbs and metabolic system. Through this equilibrium between Lucifer, working from above, and Ahriman who takes hold from below, he can liberate the middle sphere of his being from the forces of the dragon through the power of Michael (its reflection) and, hence, make possible Christ's entry into the human heart. (See p. 62.)

This microcosmic Christ process within man has a correspondence in the macrocosm with the new capacity of beholding the newly reappeared land of Shamballa in the spiritual surroundings of the Earth, where the encounter with the etheric Christ becomes possible. The fullness of light which meets man here derives from the past intelligence of the Gods, with which Michael fills the land of Shamballa in our time. And the life which pervades this land comes there through the specific collaboration of Christ; for the present reappearance of the land of Shamballa is also associated with the process that Rudolf Steiner describes as the gradual arising of the 'spirit-sphere' around the Earth, which since the Mystery of Golgotha has been forming itself into a new Sun-Earth. It comes into being through the etheric bodies of those people who have taken the Christ impulse into themselves while already on the Earth no longer completely dissolving in the cosmic ether after death, thus forming the substance of the aforesaid 'spirit-sphere' around the Earth.

Rudolf Steiner here uses the same picture as in his description of Shamballa. In olden times this land gave to human beings the archetypal revelation of the spiritual world which was brought to the Earth by initiates as higher wisdom. With the ever deeper connection of humanity with the world of matter, this land disappeared from people's vision. One can also say that, with the disappearance of the primordial, atavistic clairvoyance, it became invisible. With the kindling of the new faculties which also lead to the beholding of Christ in the etheric, this land appears once more, though now not merely filled with the light of wisdom but also with new life.

Rudolf Steiner describes the arising of the spirit-sphere referred to in a similar way. What formerly lived as forces of divine life in human etheric bodies was used up through man's ever closer connection with the physical body. And if the Mystery of Golgotha had not taken place, the enfeeblement of etheric bodies would soon have led to the disintegration of physical bodies and, hence, also to the end of Earth evolution.

What occurred through the Mystery of Golgotha was an influx of new life into human etheric bodies, which after death form the spirit-sphere around the Earth mentioned above. 'Thus an impulse had to come to the Earth through which the exhausted treasure of ancient wisdom might be replenished, through which the etheric body might be endowed with new life, thus enabling the physical element—otherwise destined for decomposition—to acquire a force of incorruptibility and to be filled with an etheric body that makes it not subject to decay, that rescues it from Earth evolution. This life that pervades the etheric body is what Christ has brought ... The Christ impulse has infused man's etheric body with life, new life, after the old has been spent!' (GA 112, 5 July 1909.)

And then in the next lecture of the same cycle Rudolf Steiner describes what happens with these etheric bodies after the death of the person concerned: 'Hence ever since that time [since the Mystery of Golgotha] there has been something in man's etheric body that is not subject to death, which does not succumb to the death-forces of the Earth . . . This force [of etheric bodies which have remained intact] will form a sphere around the Earth that is in the process of becoming a Sun. A sort of spirit-sphere is forming around the Earth out of etheric bodies that have become alive.' (Ibid., 6 July 1909.)[14]

This newly forming spirit-sphere around the Earth has a direct relationship to the land of Shamballa; indeed, it is the same land in its new form, though described from a different point of view, and is based on the same process. In a later lecture Rudolf Steiner brings this enlivening of etheric bodies into a connection with the etheric Second Coming of Christ: 'The etheric body must be revitalized, and this is connected with the new revelation of Christ. Through etheric bodies being revitalized, they behold Christ.' (GA 254, 19 October 1915.) If at this point one calls to mind that Rudolf Steiner brings this new beholding of Christ into connection with the appearance of the land of Shamballa, the inner relationship of this land to the spirit-sphere around the Earth that has been described becomes obvious.

Thus Shamballa is at once the place where the etheric Christ is manifested and the location of the 'future Sun-Earth' that is being formed (GA 112, 6 July 1909), in contrast to the interior of the Earth, whence derive the forces that are opposed to this process.[15]

In this way the Christ Being and Michael meet and work together in the land of Shamballa. Michael brings to it the light of the past intelligence of the Gods, which no longer has anything luciferic about it. And Christ brings the whole future of the cosmos in a manner such that the ahrimanic powers can no longer gain access to it.[16] At a higher level there is an encounter here between the cosmic forces of knowledge (Michael) and life (Christ), which came to expression in the imagination of the two intertwined trees.[17]

As in the macrocosm, so does Michael also interact with man in the microcosm—in order to protect his freedom—only as a model, that is, through his reflection in man's being. As we have already seen, the power of reflection in man's etheric body enables the spiritual space to arise in the heart from which all dragon forces are removed, so that a conscious encounter with the etheric Christ becomes possible.

A further process also belongs to this. In the second chapter it was already mentioned that through the development of the new, 'intellectual clairvoyance', that is, through the spiritualizing of his intellectuality, man will in our time come to a conscious perception of the etheric Christ. Michael gives man a mighty impulse towards this transformation of thinking. 'He liberates thought from the sphere of the head; he clears the way for it to the heart ... The age of Michael has dawned. Hearts are beginning to have thoughts.'[18] Or, in other words, 'that the ideas of man do not merely remain "thinking", but in thought develop "sight"'.[19] And if in this way man develops 'sight' in his ideas, the first thing that comes to meet him out of the spiritual world will be the etheric Christ Himself. Thus Michael leads man to an encounter with Christ in the etheric.

If we take this account, it should not appear to us as surprising that already in 1907, in the esoteric lesson where for the first time he made an explicit reference to the Michael mystery in connection with the year 1879, Rudolf Steiner also initially broached the theme of the etheric Second Coming of Christ. For the two events are inseparably connected with one another. Rudolf Steiner's exact words about the Second Coming were as follows: 'And as in former times, the light of the Spirit will shine brightly and radiantly into the darkness: the Christ will appear again on Earth, albeit in a different form from before. We are entrusted with the task of receiving Him and serving Him.' (GA 266/1, 5 December 1907.) And in the same esoteric lesson Rudolf Steiner says of Michael himself: 'He is the radiant Sun, which enables esoteric wisdom to ray forth into a small group of people' (ibid.) which will be gradually prepared by this new spiritual wisdom so as 'to receive and serve' the etheric Christ.

Thus these two themes appear for the first time simultaneously as though out of the background of the whole of Rudolf Steiner's anthroposophical activity, in order then, five and a half years later, to be presented to public attention on 2 May 1913 in London. For in this special lecture Rudolf Steiner spoke—with unprecedented intensity— both about the modern Michael mystery and about the second, super-sensible Mystery of Golgotha, which he calls the spiritual starting point of the ensuing appearance of Christ in the etheric. Here, too, these two events are inseparably connected with one another: Michael's incipient rulership and the new 'Christ consciousness' which was to emerge from within it from the twentieth century onwards. (See further in chapter 7.) 'This ... will gradually find its way into human souls, and the mediator, the emissary, will be Michael, who is now the ambassador of Christ' (GA 152). For the source of the new Christ consciousness is the supersensible Mystery of Golgotha. But the being who brings this knowledge to consciousness in individual human souls is Michael. 'Just as he formerly guided human souls towards an understanding of Christ's unfolding journey from heaven to Earth, so is he now preparing mankind to become capable of experiencing the emergence of the Christ con-sciousness from the realm of the unknown into that of the known' (ibid.).

Thus in our time these two beings, the Time Spirit Michael and Christ, whose countenance Michael has been since the Mystery of Golgotha, are working so intimately together that Rudolf Steiner can refer to them as *one* being. 'Thus the Michael experience and the Christ experience will ... be able to stand side by side ... *Michael-Christ* will stand in future as the guiding word at the entrance to the path upon which man may arrive at his world-goal, in a way that is cosmically right, between the luciferic and the ahrimanic powers.'[20]

In this way Rudolf Steiner links the collaboration of Christ and Michael in the present with the sculptural Group of the Representative of Man between Lucifer and Ahriman. From this it also becomes apparent why the sculptural Group can be called a kind of 'Michaelic Trinity' for our time, whose essential nature Rudolf Steiner directly connects with the present activity of Michael. In the lecture where these weighty words appear about the modern knowledge of Christ—'You must realize that the Christ impulse can be understood only if one views it as the balancing impulse between the ahrimanic and the luciferic elements, if one gives it its right place within the trinity' (GA 194, 21 November 1919)—there follows a summary of what has been presented here: 'All this is connected with the mission of Michael in relation to those beings of the higher hierarchies with whom he has been engaged—if we would but reach towards him—in transmitting an understanding of the Christ impulse in the true sense of the word' (ibid., 23 November 1919).

The sculptural Group as a present revelation of Michael also enables us to look at the sculptural composition of the First Goetheanum with different eyes. Thus in the East one sees the figure of the Representative of Man overcoming the adversarial powers, and in the West, in the red glass window, the countenance of a human being who has awoken to the new clairvoyance (he has fully developed lotus flowers) and bears within his heart the *likeness* of Michael (which is why it is so small). This likeness liberates the inner space of the heart from the forces of the dragon, so that the human individual can experience the encounter with the etheric Christ.

Thus they make their way towards one another: Christ from the East[21] and, from the West, the modern human being who has risen to the new clairvoyance with the power of Michael in his heart. And when they meet in the two spaces of the First Goetheanum (like passing through the two chambers of the human heart)[22] man can receive from Christ the power to counteract the adversarial powers as is depicted in the central motif of the sculptural Group.[23] And the important task that confronts man today is to open up the middle realm—that of the heart—to the forces of the

Christ. For 'what will bring inner logic, inner wisdom, a sense of orientation into this middle part of our human nature? The Christ impulse, that which flowed into Earth culture through the Mystery of Giolgotha.' (GA 194, 28 November 1919.) And Rudolf Steiner concludes his line of thought by summarizing it as follows: 'It is a requisite part of our human nature that we imbue ourselves with the Christ impulse' (ibid.).

Man needs this Christ impulse, the Christ power today, above all in order to endure the arduous trials that are still to befall him in the epoch of the etheric Second Coming. (Some of these will be described in the next chapter.) For this higher power, which can unshakably withstand all evil, can be attained today only through man's conscious connection with *Michael-Christ*.

6. The Second Coming and the Occult Powers that Oppose It

If one is fully conscious of the fact that Christ's appearance in the etheric is the *most important* event of our time, one will not be surprised that the adversarial powers are trying everything they can to prevent it from fully coming into effect. In order to achieve their dark goals, however, they make particular use of people living on the Earth; for neither the adversarial powers nor human beings, not even initiates—however high their level of initiation—can influence the event itself. 'The path taken by Christ Himself lies completely beyond the will and intentions of human beings. Thus no person, however knowledgeable he may be—and no initiate—has influence over what Christ does towards bringing about in the course of the twentieth century the appearance of which I have often spoken to you and of which you will also find indications in the mystery plays. This depends completely on Christ Himself. Christ will be present in the etheric sphere as an etheric Being.' (GA 178, 18 November 1917.)

Nevertheless, something can be achieved by the adversarial powers and their human servants through preventing the perceiving of the etheric Second Coming, which can have dire consequences; for something of great magnitude would indeed be involved here, namely mankind's link with the whole future evolution of the Earth, which is associated with the Jupiter condition. If mankind were in our time to miss the etheric Second Coming, it would on Jupiter likewise not have the possibility of rightly perceiving Christ's impending manifestation then and of carrying human evolution forward in accordance with the Christ impulse.[1]

In order to understand this situation better, one must call to mind the perspective of the etheric Second Coming which was given in the first chapter, that is, that Christ's appearance in the etheric is only the first stage of His triple revelation. If one proceeds on the basis that these revelations will each last 3000 years (Rudolf Steiner gives this indication for the first), they together encompass the rest of the present fifth post-Atlantean cultural epoch, which will lead to mankind's transition to the sixth great Earth period beginning after the War of All against All. If, moreover, one takes into consideration that in the fifth epoch above all man's ego is to be developed, in order in the sixth to receive the revelation of the Spirit Self as a preparation for the coming Jupiter, in the seventh that of the Life Spirit and—after the great War—the forces of the Spirit Man, it follows that the perceiving of the etheric appearance of Christ today must bring about the decisive step for *this entire* future evolution, that is, the transition from the individual ego to the first dawning of the Spirit Self, or from intellectual thinking to the perceiving of the spiritual world and of Christ Himself in conscious imaginations.

The sequence of the three supersensible revelations of Christ, beginning in our time with the etheric Second Coming, is also of decisive significance from another aspect. For whereas His present revelation on the astral plane seeks to lead human beings into the spiritual world through the new, imaginative clairvoyance, His second revelation (the appearance in the astral body in Lower Devachan) will prepare humanity rightly to approach the Earth's union with the Moon, which will take place in the eighth millennium of our era.[2]

In accordance with this Christ-rhythm, His third revelation (as the World Ego in Higher Devachan) then brings us to the sixth great period of the Earth, when its union with the Sun of Christ Himself is prepared. Thus the present experience of Christ in the etheric on the part of humanity can be understood as the starting point of the whole evolutionary sequence which has been described, culminating in the union of the Earth with the Sun and then its transition to the Jupiter condition, which in turn will also form the foundation for the further aeons of Venus and Vulcan.

If one considers this briefly sketched perspective more closely, one may well suppose that—as already mentioned—active preparations are being made from various sides to oppose the etheric Second Coming. Rudolf Steiner refers directly to some such counter-movements and describes them in detail, while others can be inferred indirectly from his various spiritual-scientific indications. To begin with he speaks in this respect about the diametrically opposed Western and Eastern occult lodges. The former belong primarily to the English-speaking peoples of the world. The latter are of Indo-Tibetan origin. Both have—albeit in different ways—secret occult-political plans through which they strive for world-rulership. The Western lodges—Rudolf Steiner also calls them the secret brotherhoods of the West or simply 'evil brotherhoods' (GA 178, 18 November 1917)—seek to achieve their group interests above all through politics and economic activity; whereas the Eastern brotherhoods hope to achieve theirs through the dissemination of their age-old spirituality which—while no longer appropriate for the present—they have preserved from time immemorial. Both parties employ, in addition to outward, exoteric means, also occult ones, which Rudolf Steiner has discovered and precisely described. He has done this above all because only knowledge of their obscure machinations is capable of breaking the occult power of these dark lodges. It can almost be taken for granted that both these parties in our time direct their particular efforts against the etheric Second Coming, which alone can bring their claims to authority to an inglorious end.

Thus Rudolf Steiner reports from his spiritual research that at the centre of the occult activities of the Western brotherhoods is the mystery of 'ahrimanic immortality' (GA 174, 22 January 1917).[3] This will also be used to strengthen the growing spread of materialism (Rudolf Steiner indicates that this will intensify until the middle of the fifth cultural epoch)[4] by making it occult, as such lodge members who try to extend their influence across the threshold of death endeavour to do. Through certain rituals of ceremonial magic it is made possible for dead members of the lodge or people who during their earthly life have in one way or another fallen under its influence to be held back after their death in the realm of this lodge and of the ahrimanic spirits who inspire it in the spiritual world. Thus the forces of the dead are used for the questionable purposes of the lodge's leadership, thus bringing about a considerable enlarging of the power and sphere of influence of such an occult brotherhood.

All this has from the outset an expressly hostile attitude to Christ, even an antichristian character; for the people who stand at the apex of such lodges and aspire to the ahrimanic immortality referred to are utterly convinced that the world of ahrimanic spirits by whom they are inspired and guided and with whose help they hope to attain their power-political aims is stronger than the sphere of Christ. Hence the brothers who are at the head of these lodges say to themselves: 'We do not want Christ to be our guide, Christ who is the guide for the normal world; we want a different guide, for we want to oppose this normal world' (ibid.). And then Rudolf Steiner explains to his listeners, who must quite understandably have experienced such intentions as 'somewhat incomprehensible', how something of this sort can be inherently possible: 'They [the brothers who guide the lodges] gain from the preparations that they undergo . . . from the preparations brought about by ceremonial magic, the impression that the world of ahrimanic powers is a far more powerful spiritual world [than the world of Christ] and that it will above all enable them to continue what they have achieved here in the physical world, namely that they are able to make the material experiences of physical life immortal' (ibid.). Rudolf Steiner also says that the 'ahrimanic powers' referred to here are 'Archai who have remained at the stage of Archangeloi', and are 'in the strongest sense imbued with ahrimanic influences'.

These shadowy brotherhoods want to appropriate and misuse the leading role which in our fifth cultural epoch has been allotted to the English-speaking people of the world—as representatives of the consciousness soul—by the good powers guiding the world for their power-political aims through the world-wide strengthening of materialism.[5] The goal which is of primal importance to them in this respect is to keep this fifth post-Atlantean epoch going for all eternity, so as to render the transition to the sixth period and to the entire further evolution of humanity and the Earth impossible.[6] 'Those brotherhoods of whom I have spoken have—to the exclusive benefit of their egoistic group-interests—set themselves the task of making the fifth post-Atlantean period into the entire endeavour of earthly evolution and eliminating what ought to flow into this earthly evolution in the sixth and seventh post-Atlantean periods' (ibid.).

Rudolf Steiner describes in addition how concretely these brotherhoods are working today against Christ's Second Coming. They cannot prevent this event, but they try to make it imperceptible for people, especially by drawing their attention to another being appearing in the etheric whom they themselves serve. 'These brotherhoods of which I have just spoken, which wish to confine the souls of human beings [after their death] to the materialistic sphere, aim to ensure that Christ will pass by unnoticed in the twentieth century, that His coming as an etheric individuality will be unobserved by people. This endeavour of theirs develops under the influence of a quite definite idea, under a definite impulse of will; for these brotherhoods have the urge to conquer the sphere of influence that should come through Christ in the twentieth century and on into the future ... for another being. There are brotherhoods of the West whose aim it is to dispute the validity of Christ's impulse and to put another individuality who has never yet appeared in the flesh but is only an etheric individuality, though of a strongly ahrimanic nature, in His place' (GA 178, 18 November 1917). And then come the decisive words: 'All those measures about which I have just spoken regarding the dead and so forth ultimately serve the aim of leading people away from Christ, who passed through the Mystery of Golgotha, and of securing the *rulership of the Earth* for another individuality' (ibid.).

From this it follows that what is at issue here is nothing less than the rulership of the whole Earth, which is handed over by human beings themselves to Christ or to the being who can be characterized as having 'aspirations that are in the strongest sense antichristian' (ibid.). And Rudolf Steiner adds to what he is saying with great seriousness: 'It is a real struggle which is indeed concerned with putting another being in the Christ

Being's place in the course of mankind's evolution for the rest of the fifth post-Atlantean period and for the sixth and seventh' (ibid.).

In the battle which must be fought in this domain and in which anthroposophists, because of the fundamental knowledge that Rudolf Steiner has imparted to them, have an important role to play, there is a particular difficulty in that the members of these brotherhoods mis-appropriate the holy Name for the being whom they want to put in the place of the etheric Christ. 'For the other being whom these brother-hoods want to make the ruler [of the Earth] they will call "Christ"; they will indeed give him the name of "Christ"' (ibid.).

A similar question to this is as though prophetically portrayed in a Russian heroic epic tale. There alongside the ahrimanic being of 'anti-truth' ('Krivda') someone suddenly appears whom the Russian warriors consider to be Christ but who is then unmasked by the Archangel Michael as the Antichrist.[7] This situation can become for us the key to recognize the nature of this ahrimanic etheric individuality out of anthroposophy—which Rudolf Steiner in one context calls the 'gift of Michael' (GA 152, 2 May 1913)—and to warn human beings in general about him. For this individuality can be distinguished from Christ in one particular respect, in that he has never—as did Christ at the Turning Point of Time—lived on Earth in an earthly incarnation. (See GA 178, 18 November 1917.)

However, the mystery of the identity of this 'eminently ahrimanic' and antichristian being is not unveiled in the lecture that has been cited. However, one can draw some conclusions from other indications that Rudolf Steiner has given. Thus he describes one year later how around the year 666 of our era the attempt was made to unleash a mighty ahri-manic impulse against the entire evolution which will follow the con-sciousness soul, an impulse emanating from the apocalyptic beast from the abyss through the Academy of Gondhishapur and extending throughout the whole civilized world at that time. This was to happen through the consciousness soul, which was intended to extend its sway over the Earth only from the beginning of the fifteenth century (1413), being initiated already in the seventh century as a purely ahrimanic revelation by that being whom Rudolf Steiner calls the Sun demon or the cosmic opponent of Christ. By this means Sorat (for that is the name of the Sun demon) wanted to achieve the following: 'He [man] was to remain at the level of the consciousness soul, he was to retain what the Earth can give him but no more, he was not to go on to the evolutions of Jupiter, Venus and Vulcan ... This was to be prevented. Hence human individuals were to receive the consciousness soul and all that belongs to it earlier [that is, in the seventh century] through its being infiltrated or injected into the intellectual or mind soul. Then man would have remained in his development at the level of the consciousness soul; he would be an automaton awash with the knowledge which would flow towards him from the sixth age onwards! But then there would be nothing more that he could do; he would not develop further, save to assimilate knowledge into his consciousness soul, placing it all with the utmost egotism at the service of the consciousness soul.' (GA 184, 11 October 1918.)

One can see from this description that what in our time and in a different way the evil brotherhoods of the West aspire towards was to be achieved at that time by Sorat on a more extensive scale. Whereas in the seventh century Sorat tried to render the whole future evolution of the world (Jupiter, Venus and Vulcan) impossible, the Western brotherhoods in our time intend to prevent the inauguration of those cultural epochs amongst mankind which have the task as though prophetically to prepare this future evolution: the sixth cultural epoch (Jupiter), the seventh (Venus) and the sixth great period (Vulcan).[8]

Where it concerns the future of the whole cosmic evolutionary journey, the transition from the fifth to the sixth cultural epoch is in both cases of decisive significance. This is why some highly important conflicts regarding human evolution will take place around this time, for which spiritual science must prepare people already now. (See GA 159/160, 15 June 1915.)

In the seventh century Sorat was unable to achieve his aim because of the ongoing effects of the Mystery of Golgotha. Now he is making a renewed attempt and wants to make up his lost ground through the aforesaid brotherhoods. But he will only succeed if he can manage to make humanity fail to notice the coming of the etheric Christ.

With this we are touching upon a mystery which initially seems to be a contradiction. For in the lecture from which the quotation has been made about the impulse of Gondhishapur Rudolf Steiner calls Sorat a 'being of an ahrimanic nature' (ibid.).[9] In the cycle on the Book of Revelation from 1908, however, he is called the Sun demon and the greatest opponent of Christ Himself, who in his essential nature belongs not—as do the ahrimanic powers—to earthly evolution but intervenes into it from yonder worlds as the true Antichrist. The contradiction is, however, resolved if one bears in mind that Sorat, because he comes from outside earthly evolution, can only be active within it through the mediation of other beings who belong to it. Thus he manifested his power in the seventh century through the mediation of a leading ahrimanic being who inspired the seductive wisdom of Gondhishapur as though from behind and would even—if the experiment had succeeded—himself 'have appeared, albeit not on the physical plane' (ibid.). Thus already then there was a kind of etheric manifestation of this 'strongly ahrimanic' being who serves Sorat and represents him in earthly evolution.

It is likewise this latter being whom in our time we find chosen by the brotherhoods of the West to take the place of the etheric Christ in the spiritual world bordering on the Earth, in order to make humanity question the existence of the etheric Christ. This is a being who, as Sorat's emissary, 'incarnates only as far as the etheric and is to be put by these brotherhoods in the place of Christ, who is to pass by unobserved' (GA 178, 18 November 1917).

If we add to what has been said here something that we also know through Rudolf Steiner, namely that the Bolshevik Revolution in Russia in the autumn of 1917 was clearly staged and carried out by the Bolsheviks as a 'socialist experiment' undertaken by these brotherhoods of the West,[10] we will understand still better what Rudolf Steiner meant when he spoke of the Bolsheviks as 'people of Sorat'. 'The Sorat people will also be recognizable by their external appearance; they will in the most terrible way not only scoff at everything but also oppose and want to push into the mire anything that is of a spiritual nature. This will be experienced, for example, in the way that something that is concentrated into a small space in seed form as today's Bolshevism will become incorporated into the whole evolution of humanity.' (GA 346, 12 September 1924.)[11]

It follows from this that what was prepared in the Western lodges out of Sorat's inspiration (through the aforesaid ahrimanic being) found its first fulfilment in that country which has the task of laying the foundation for the sixth cultural epoch and, hence, for the whole further evolution of the Earth; for as the 'Christ people'[12] the Russian people (and in an additional sense the whole Slavic population of Europe) not only has the task of founding the sixth epoch but also bears within itself—and in a quite particular way—the forces for the new clairvoyance and for perceiving the etheric Christ.[13] It was this that was to be thoroughly eradicated through the 'export' of Bolshevism from the West. How things stand after the fall of Bolshevism and to what extent the 70-year-long Bolshevik terror succeeded in destroying these tender, supersensible faculties in the souls of Russian people must be left open here; for a final judgement about this can be made only in the future.

Mankind's decision as to which way it wants to proceed with regard to the etheric Second Coming must, however, be taken out of the free individual ego in the fifth cultural epoch. Hence Rudolf Steiner always speaks of how this epoch is of immeasurable importance as the time of great decisions, which is of significance for the whole of earthly evolution.[14]

★

The Eastern brotherhoods, in particular those of a left orientation, work in a completely different way, though with no less vehemence, against the etheric appearance of Christ. Because of the particular nature of their spirituality they do not work with dead souls (for Eastern incarnations do not give people sufficient forces to maintain their ego-consciousness after death, as is possible for people of the West) but with completely different, though no less problematic occult forces. As we know from anthroposophy, during the first three days after a person's death his etheric body separates from the astral body and ego. This etheric body will normally be received by the cosmic ether and be dissolved in it. However, these Eastern brotherhoods have certain occult methods by means of which they preserve the etheric bodies of individuals who belonged to such a lodge or brotherhood during their life for a longer time before dissolution. These etheric bodies of the dead which are artificially bound to the spiritual world bordering upon the Earth can then be taken over by demons of a particular kind who have a connection with such lodges. 'Thus the Western lodges have the dead who have been directly confined within matter; the Eastern lodges with a left orientation have demonic spirits, spirits who do not belong to earthly evolution but creep into it by occupying the etheric bodies vacated by human beings' (GA 178, 18 November 1917). Demons who 'do not belong to earthly evolution' are primarily those who are directly answerable to Sorat in the spiritual world.

Through these occult manipulations the Eastern brotherhoods try above all to prevent 'the Mystery of Golgotha with its impulse from taking hold of the evolution of humanity. They ... do not want this' (ibid.). Thus they seek in this dubious manner to counteract the etheric manifestation of Christ, so that 'when Christ as an individuality passes over the Earth [in the etheric body] He remains unnoticed ...' (ibid.). And how can they achieve this with the etheric bodies of the dead inhabited by Sorat's demons? Rudolf Steiner answers this question by means of an example deriving from a completely different situation. On the Earth there are nations whose natural tendency is to mould a person's etheric body in so strongly national a way that after death it will take far longer to dissolve than the etheric bodies of other nations. If something of this kind happens, such an etheric body—especially if its possessor has shown no inclination towards the spiritual world in his last earthly life— can be used by the adversarial powers to assist in distorting the imagination of the etheric Christ in our time in such a way that the danger arises that 'Christ [will] appear in a false form, in false imaginations' (GA 158, 9 November 1914). And if this tendency manifests itself in ordinary—though somewhat hardened—etheric bodies of dead people, this is almost immeasurably increased if such an etheric body is, through the machinations of the brotherhoods referred to, taken possession of by a demon serving Sorat who has implanted itself in this etheric body. Thus the undissolved etheric bodies of the dead are used by demons serving Sorat as a powerful means of working in the manner indicated against the purity of the image in which the etheric Christ must appear.

This is the mystery that is familiar to the Eastern brotherhoods. Hence they try through such Sorat demons as inhabit etheric bodies to distort the imagination of the etheric Christ to the extent that people no longer pay it proper attention and consider it to be something else. In order to confuse them even further in this respect, in some regions of Asia a kind of demonized 'ancestor worship'—developed by the same lodges—is disseminated and promoted which aims to replace the true perception of the etheric Christ. People speak in this respect of ancestors, but they actually mean the demons working through the etheric bodies of the dead. Rudolf Steiner describes it thus: 'The ancestor is simply the one who has laid aside his etheric body, which has been occupied by demons through the machinations of the lodge. So the veneration of ancestors is brought about. But these ancestors who are being worshipped are simply demonic beings in the etheric body of the ancestor in question.' (GA 178, 18 November 1917.) This is how the Eastern lodges work against the etheric Second Coming today: 'By this means their purpose will be achieved, namely that Christ as an [etheric] individuality—as He is intended to pass over the Earth—remains unnoticed by Eastern people *and perhaps by people everywhere*' (ibid.). And then Rudolf Steiner adds by way of a summary: 'Thus in a certain sense a battle is being waged today from two sides [by the Western and Eastern lodges] against the Christ impulse appearing in the etheric in the course of the twentieth century' (ibid.).

★

In addition to Bolshevism, which manifested itself in its full force and with the destructive power of the Russian Revolution and which Rudolf Steiner characterized as a consequence of the influence of the Sorat demons amongst human beings, there was in the same century a second mighty attack by Sorat, this time in Central Europe, in Adolf Hitler's accession to power in 1933. It is deeply moving today to read the words in which in September 1924 Rudolf Steiner as though prophetically refers in the cycle on the Book of Revelation, given to the priests of the Christian Community, to the whole occult dimension of this event in the history of Germany and brings the whole phenomenon into a connection with the etheric Second Coming: 'Before the etheric Christ can be comprehended by human beings in the right way, humanity must first cope with encountering the beast who will rise up in 1933' (GA 346, 20 September 1924).[15]

In the ensuing twelve years this battle with the beast from the abyss, with the Sorat demon himself, raged not only in Germany but on the soil of virtually the whole of Europe, in a manner which in its horror and cruelty far exceeded anything that had previously happened in the history of mankind. The question which, however, initially remained unanswered was to what extent the process of Christ's appearance in the etheric was prevented by this. The importance of this question is intensified by the following.

Everyone who is familiar with Rudolf Steiner's observations about the Second Coming will be immediately struck by the fact that he always indicates the same period for the beginning of this process: from 1930 until 1945,[16] which precisely corresponds to the time of the horrific domination of National Socialism, a movement which brought the greatest conceivable obstacles to the coming of the etheric Christ. And these obstacles arose first and foremost in the country to which shortly before, as the culmination and highest blossoming of its hundreds of years of cultural development, anthroposophy had been given as a new language with which people of today can pose their most important questions to the etheric Christ. (See regarding this in chapter 2.)

Thus one can wholly agree with the conclusion that the anthroposophical historian Karl Heyer (1888–1964) came to after his lifelong study of the historical and esoteric foundations of National Socialism, namely that the National Socialist movement was none other than an 'anti-anthroposophical movement'.[17]

From what has been said it becomes clear that in this respect the destiny of the Germans is wholly comparable with that of the Russians in the twentieth century. Both were by virtue of their natural disposition entrusted with playing an important part in the initial stirrings of the etheric Second Coming. The Germans had the task of conveying to humanity by means of their gift of anthroposophy the message of the etheric Christ as the most important of our time; and the Russians, who were called by Rudolf Steiner the 'Christ people', were to manifest a particular sensitivity and receptiveness for these tidings. For the etheric Second Coming, which has begun in the twentieth century and will last for three thousand years, is to reach its culmination in the first half of the sixth cultural epoch, which must be established by the Slavs, and permeate the whole of cultural development as a central spiritual impulse.

But, as already said, no power in the world (not even Sorat) can stop the etheric Second Coming. However, placing obstacles in its path, which consists in diverting human beings from this event, has indeed happened in a far-reaching way—in the twentieth century pre-eminently through the appearance of Bolshevism and National Socialism on the stage of world history. Nevertheless, this does not in any way represent the end of the battle concerning the appearance of the etheric Christ, nor has it already been won by the adversarial powers. It continues; and anthroposophists, who have the greatest knowledge about it in our time, will have an important task with respect to its possible outcome during the next three thousand years. Moreover, this task remains a living reality, even if the inner consequences of Sorat's assault on Central and Eastern Europe in the twentieth century will not be able to be properly appreciated for a long time.

In the context of this chapter, however, it is of significance to state that there is a kind of collaboration between the secret brotherhoods of the West and the East. Meanwhile, the help that National Socialism—and the ensuing Hitler regime—received from the West as it was emerging is already generally known.[18] The connections zealously forged by the Nazis with the Himalayas and the secret knowledge of the East still preserved there have also long been a familiar fact.[19] The positive estimations of Hitler and his regime appearing again and again in the East can also be understood in this context.[20] Ultimately it was a question of doing away with Christianity amidst the widest possible extension of the power of the National Socialists (as was intended through the World War) and of everywhere establishing neo-pagan cults of Arian origin with a kind of ancestor worship at their centre, as practised by Eastern brotherhoods of a left persuasion.[21]

In the same way and no less radically, an abolition of Christianity was envisaged by the leaders of the Bolshevik regime. In particular, any soul foundation for the continuing effectiveness of the 'Christ people' in Eastern Europe was to be destroyed with the creation of the 'new man' in the sense of Bolshevik ideology. The model of the 'socialist experiment' imported from the West was associated in Russia with an increasingly strong Asiatic heritage[22] and was to be disseminated throughout the world as a uniquely effective destructive force. Historically, the relationship of the Bolshevik Government to the Eastern brotherhoods is indicated in the famous Mahatma letter, which Nicholas and Helena Roerich brought 'from the heights of the Himalayas' at the end of the 1920s to the government then already led by Stalin. In this document the Bolshevik regime in Russia was fully and without any qualification affirmed and supported by the mahatmas.[23]

All these facts bear witness that the endeavours of the Western and Eastern brotherhoods of a left persuasion are going in the same direction as those of the Sorat demons and of Sorat himself. They are working together against Christ's appearance in the etheric, as could be seen in the twentieth century through the unholy alliance of Bolshevism and National Socialism.

★

During the ten years of his involvement with the Theosophical Society (1902–12), Rudolf Steiner had a perfect opportunity to observe the activities and occult methods of the Eastern lodges from a very close vantage-point. Furthermore, because of his uncompromising adherence to Christian-Rosicrucian occultism, he had to engage in an arduous dispute in this regard in order to protect the impending appearance of Christ in the etheric.

For this reason it is necessary to address this theme again and at greater length. Earlier on in this chapter it has already been mentioned how the hardened etheric bodies of human individuals dissolve only with difficulty after their death and, hence, can be used to oppose Christ's etheric Second Coming. In such a case Michael likewise has to battle together with the human souls belonging to him for the undistorted appearance of the etheric Christ. (See GA 158, 9 November 1914.) But he has a far harder battle to fight against etheric bodies possessed by the demons of Sorat such as are worked with in the Eastern lodges and who in a similar way, though far more forcefully, try to oppose the etheric Second Coming; for there is a distinct difference between the two kinds of etheric body. Hardened etheric bodies[24] that have arisen in the normal course of evolution only bring about a distortion of the imagination of Christ—which can be corrected by the good spirits. However, etheric bodies possessed by Sorat's demons already have the power to bring this imagination so far towards obliteration that people on Earth will no longer notice it at all. The wave of Indo-Tibetan occultism that is extending its sway in our time over the entire world must be viewed from the standpoint indicated here. The aspirations of the left-oriented Eastern lodges referred to above stand behind a large number—though not all—of the movements of this nature, even though the individuals who are outwardly disseminating this Eastern occultism initially have no idea of their secret aims.

The following words written by Rudolf Steiner make it apparent that this is a very serious situation which could ultimately have a gravely damaging effect on the influence of the Christ impulse amongst mankind: 'For the Eastern initiations must of necessity leave untouched the *Christ principle* as the central *cosmic* factor of evolution ... They could only hope for success within evolution if the principle of Christianity were to be eradicated from Western culture. But this would be the same as eradicating the essential *meaning of the Earth*, which lies in the recognition and realization of the intentions of the *living Christ*.' (GA 262, The Barr Manuscript, part III; italics Rudolf Steiner.)

Michael, together with the human souls belonging to him, is battling today against such etheric bodies, which as a result of the manipulations of the Eastern lodges are possessed by Soratic demons. In this battle the entelechy of the sister soul of Adam mentioned in chapter 1 and the Archangel Vidar stand at his side. The latter in particular plays a decisive role in this battle, for it is his task to work contrary to any kind of atavistic clairvoyance,[25] where the imagination of the Second Coming can only appear in a distorted form.

A further danger, which Rudolf Steiner has only indicated, has its source in these and similar manipulations of the Eastern lodges. These work contrary not only to the etheric Second Coming but also just as assiduously to the consequences of what entered into humanity through the Mystery of Golgotha at the Turning Point of Time. These left-oriented Eastern brotherhoods with their age-old spirituality are altogether antagonistic to the Christ impulse. They do everything 'to divert [people's] interest from this Christ; they—these Eastern, and specifically Indian, brotherhoods—do not want to let Christianity make any further progress. They do not want any interest to develop in the real Christ who passed through the Mystery of Golgotha, who was for three years here on Earth in a unique incarnation and who can no longer appear in an earthly incarnation.' (GA 178, 18 November 1917.)

These words of Rudolf Steiner clearly show that the Eastern brotherhoods do not want to accept the uniqueness of Christ's incarnation and, hence, the central significance of the Mystery of Golgotha for the whole of Earth evolution. It is this that allures them into believing that Christ, whom they regard as one of many bodhisattvas known from history, will—also after the Turning Point of Time—appear again and again on the Earth in a physical body. Out of this conviction a second mighty onslaught is being prepared by the Eastern brotherhoods, which is directed both against the Mystery of Golgotha and the appearance of the etheric Christ. For the Eastern brotherhoods know that were Christ to appear in a physical body on Earth even only once after the Turning Point of Time He would Himself have obliterated His deed on Golgotha. Hence the most effective way of campaigning against the Mystery of Golgotha and diverting people's attention from Christ's appearance in the etheric is to proclaim on a world-wide basis that He has reappeared in a physical body.

In the history of the Theosophical Society it was *these* intentions of the left-oriented Eastern brotherhoods which appeared shortly after its founding. Rudolf Steiner indicated as such especially in a series of lectures that he gave in 1915, during the First World War. That he harboured no illusions in this regard is evident from the words from the Barr Manuscript which he had written already in 1907.

Rudolf Steiner sums up the occult history of the founder of the Theosophical Society, H.P. Blavatsky, as follows. After the original Eastern initiates whom she had originally inspired and led had withdrawn,[26] pseudo-mahatmas appeared in their stead who either had a connection to the brotherhoods in question or, still more likely, were themselves members of them. Through this unhealthy influence Blavatsky's soul, occultly prepared by her new guides, gradually became a hater of Christ. This could only happen through her being impregnated with the idea that Lucifer, rather than Jehovah, is mankind's greatest benefactor. Rudolf Steiner gives the following account of this: 'In order to do something herself that would outweigh what Sinnett was saying,[27] she [Blavatsky] agreed to the proposals of the Indian occultists who were inspiring her.[28] These occultists, being adherents of the left path, had no other aim than the promotion of their own special—Indian—interests. Their aim was to establish all over the Earth a system of wisdom from which Christ, and Yahweh (Jehovah) too, were excluded. Therefore something had to be interpolated into the theory which gradually eliminated Christ and Jehovah. The following means were adopted [by the Eastern occultists of a left persuasion]. It was said [to Blavatsky and her followers]: look at Lucifer (they didn't mention Ahriman; so little was known about him that the same name was used *for both*), this Lucifer [and also Ahriman] is mankind's great benefactor. He brings people everything that they have through their head: science, art, in short all progress. He is the true spirit of light, he is the one to follow. As for Jehovah, what has he actually done? He established the principle of physical heredity among human beings! He is a Moon God, who introduced a Moon influence . . . This shines through the entire structure of [Blavatsky's] *Secret Doctrine* and is, moreover, clearly stated there. Hence for occult reasons H.P. Blavatsky was prepared in such a way as to become a hater of Christ and Jehovah.' (GA 254, 18 October 1915.)

However, since Blavatsky outwardly needed to take Christianity into account (for her intention was to spread her teaching pre-eminently in the Western world), she had somehow to integrate its founder into her occult system, which was now inspired by left-oriented Eastern brotherhoods. She did this by equating Christ Jesus with Jeshu ben Pandira, who had lived approximately one hundred years before (also in Palestine), and receiving Him into the circle of theosophical Masters as one of the bodhisattvas. What was merely indicated by Blavatsky herself was fully formulated by her successor, Annie Besant.[29] However, the basic error of the whole theosophical doctrine—confusing Jesus of Nazareth with Jeshu ben Pandira—goes back to Blavatsky and her occult inspirations.[30]

With this distorted foundation it was only a question of time when Annie Besant would—out of the same inspirations of the left-oriented brothers hovering in the background—publicly proclaim Christ as a reincarnating bodhisattva and, hence, as the future World Teacher. Shortly afterwards the corresponding human vessel for the future World Teacher—the incarnated Maitreya-Christ—was found by her colleague C.W. Leadbeater. After the failure of his attempt with the Dutch boy Hubert van Hook, in 1909 he finally discovered the Indian boy Krishnamurti.[31]

In the present context, it is especially the year when the mischief surrounding Krishnamurti as the World Teacher and incarnated Christ began its work which is of significance. Leadbeater, who engineered the whole deception, probably—despite his clairvoyance—knew far less about the mystery of the year 1909 than the left-oriented Eastern occultists who inspired him. For a *Christian* initiate—in this case Rudolf Steiner—was able precisely in 1909 to perceive the etheric Christ for the first time within the astral sphere of the Earth. Thus His etheric appearance coincides with the attempt to make Him imperceptible to human individuals by instituting the false Christ as the World Teacher through the Theosophical Society.

We know from the subsequent history that Rudolf Steiner's opposition in principle to this occult deception led in 1912 to his and his friends' expulsion from the Theosophical Society, whereupon an independent Anthroposophical Society could be established already at Christmas 1912 in Cologne. The entire episode is summed up in these words of Rudolf Steiner, which necessarily apply not only to that time but also to the full three thousand years of the etheric Second Coming: 'False Christs will appear in this age when mankind is to see the true Christ in the etheric body. But anthroposophists are under the obligation to be able to distinguish between the spiritual and the material and to be solidly armed against all assertions—wherever they may come from—that a Christ would come in the flesh. Anthroposophists are expected to have the insight that this would be sheer materialism, the deadliest tempter who could appear amidst one of the most important events of human evolution, the event that we call Christ's Second Coming' (GA 118, 30 January 1910).[32]

Similarly in the so-called little apocalypse on the Mount of Olives, Christ Himself referred to this in reference to our time: 'And then if anyone says to you: "Look, here is the Christ!" or "Look, there he is!" do not believe it. False Christs and false prophets will arise and show signs and wonders, to lead astray, if possible, the elect' (Mark 13:21–22).[33]

★

The seriousness of this opposition against the etheric Second Coming is apparent from two further observations by Rudolf Steiner which need to be grasped by people today in their full gravity. The Eastern name of Shamballa used in them means—in the context of the lecture from which the quotation has been made—the spiritual sphere where the etheric Christ is active today and where He would seek to lead human individuals through the development of new clairvoyant faculties. (See further about this in chapter 5.) 'Such is the great decision to be made at the parting of the ways: either downwards or upwards; either to descend to something that as a cosmic kamaloka lies deeper than Kali Yuga, or to ascend to what makes it possible for man to enter that realm which is truly alluded to by the name of Shamballa' (GA 116, 9 March 1910). If one calls to mind that a human individual will be quite particularly at the mercy of the power of demons in consequence of his evil deeds in past earthly lives at the time of kamaloka, it may be supposed that these words actually refer to the cosmic kamaloka already taking place on the Earth. This condition is prophetically described in the Revelation of St John as follows: 'And in those days men will seek death and will not find it; they will long to die, and death will fly from them' (9:6). The etheric Second Coming will then be such a horrifying prospect to human individuals that they will say 'to the mountains and rocks: "Fall on us and hide us from the face of him who is seated on the throne, and from the wrath of the Lamb"' (6:16). Rudolf Steiner also indicates that if people who have spurned the preparation offered by spiritual science are unable to understand Christ in His etheric manifestation and as the Lord of Karma, the etheric revelation will appear to them as a terrible punishment. 'For a person who looks upon it unprepared, when his [clairvoyant] powers have been awakened, will not be able to understand it [Christ's appearance in the etheric]. The Lord of

Karma will then appear to him as a terrible punishment.' (GA 131, 14 October 1911.)

A second observation by Rudolf Steiner points towards further consequences of a failure on the part of human beings to receive the etheric Christ, this time more in a temporal perspective: 'It is in this way, therefore, that we should speak of the Second Coming of Christ and of the fact that we raise ourselves up to Christ in the spiritual world by acquiring etheric vision ... Otherwise, humanity would have to wait a long, long time for such an opportunity to be repeated. It will indeed have to wait a long time, until another incarnation of the Earth' (GA 118, 25 January 1910).[34] But then Rudolf Steiner makes this awful perspective, according to which mankind will have to wait until Jupiter for a conscious collaboration with Christ,[35] even more precise, and presents a second possibility of this negative scenario which is associated with humanity's inability to perceive the Christ, plunging it inexorably into materialism, and thus leading to its being confronted by a mighty catastrophe which will encompass the entire Earth. 'If this does not succeed, the Earth will sink into materialism and mankind would have to begin anew either on the Earth itself or on the next planet [Jupiter]' (GA 118, 27 February 1910). And after these words Rudolf Steiner concludes his lecture with the great cry: 'The Earth needs anthroposophy! Whoever realizes this is an anthroposophist.' Even today anthroposophy remains the only spiritual stream which reveals these truths to human beings and indicates to them the ways in which this awful future can be avoided.

★

In summary one can say that both the left-oriented factions described, working respectively from the West and from the East, nevertheless have a common aim: to prevent the etheric Second Coming with all means available to them. The Eastern occultists try to achieve their goal above all through the appearance of a physical World Teacher, who will one day be the true Antichrist.[36] The Western occultists, on the other hand, with the same object in view make use of an ahrimanic Sorat being who dwells in the spiritual world bordering upon the Earth. Both projects, however, come together in the incarnation of Ahriman at the beginning of the third Christian millennium. It is true that he will, according to indications given by Rudolf Steiner, incarnate in North America[37] and certainly enjoy the greatest possible support of the Western brotherhoods; but he will at the same time embody that 'ideal' which the Eastern occultists of a left persuasion cherish in their circles. In other words, the approaching Ahriman will conclusively unite the Western and Eastern brotherhoods with one another in their battle against the etheric Christ and, therefore, subject the whole of humanity in both East and West to the severest possible trial in its relationship to the true Christ who is active in the etheric realm.

It can likewise be presumed that during his incarnation he will remain in constant spiritual connection with that same ahrimanic Sorat being who is supersensibly active in the Western lodges. He will quite possibly refer directly to this being as the 'Christ' who is inspiring him; and he will be spiritually surrounded and strengthened by the Sorat demons from the Eastern lodges working through the etheric bodies of the dead. Even if the incarnated Ahriman does not appear specifically as envisaged by Vladimir Solovyov as the benefactor of mankind who wins the amazement of the whole world,[38] his magical influence upon mankind and upon the whole of present civilization will be on a very considerable scale. For sometimes an influence working in the background can achieve far more than any amount of outward, visible deeds.

Out of various symptoms that Rudolf Steiner describes as belonging to the influence of the incarnated Ahriman,[39] one in particular must be referred to here. Among other things he will establish large schools of practical magic and occultism, where individuals will very quickly achieve clairvoyance without having to make any kind of spiritual or moral effort to do so. Just as in its time in the Academy of Gondhishapur all knowledge was to be imparted to the pupils as though from above and, moreover, in a form that did not correspond to the evolutionary stage of humanity at that time, it will be said to the pupils of the future school of Ahriman that they could simply remain as they are, that they do not need any spiritual or moral development to arrive at spiritual experiences, that a true inner development in the sense of the book *Knowledge of the Higher Worlds* is no longer needed for the attainment of higher faculties because more advanced methods would be offered to them here. However, the consequences of this will be that such people will after their arrival on the other side of the threshold be completely at the mercy of the ahrimanic Sorat being and the demons forming his army in the etheric bodies of the dead. A kind of mass possession of demonic beings will spread amongst mankind as a spiritual epidemic from such ahrimanic schools.

It is also the case that these occult, magical activities of Ahriman are without doubt comprehensively supported by both the brotherhoods of the West and the East; for in each of these brotherhoods people have long worked with clairvoyant powers in order in the one case to enable the etheric Sorat-like being to gain access to human individuals and, in the other, to entice them with the help of the demons working through the discarded etheric bodies of the dead in such a way as to prevent any real perception of Christ's Second Coming. Thus the magical schools that Ahriman will open throughout the world will be more than welcome to both brotherhoods for the attaining of their antichristian aims.

In this connection Rudolf Steiner refers to a significant quality of this ahrimanic clairvoyance, which will purposefully oppose the new clairvoyance that leads to an experience of the etheric Christ. Moreover, a further consequence of this ahrimanic process of gaining clairvoyance for human beings will be to distort and obscure this very experience and ultimately to replace it with its ahrimanic counterpart, so that the graduates of such ahrimanic schools perceive not the etheric Christ but the ahrimanic Sorat being in the spiritual world and, through the nature of their distorted clairvoyance, consider this being to be the Christ.

When the new, Christian clairvoyance comes to be of a nature that all people who are endowed with it sooner or later behold the same thing— Christ in the etheric—and, hence, embark upon the path of forming one great human brotherhood encompassing all divisions between nations, world-conceptions and religions that exist in our time, what might be described as an all-embracing Christ-imbued body of humanity, in the ahrimanic schools people will indeed enter the spiritual world but in such a way that everyone will see something completely different there. Through this splitting of humanity, which will exert a barely conceivable compelling power over it through coming from the supersensible world, the spiritual foundation will be laid amongst mankind for the subsequent War of All against All. For each person will be seduced by a different demon and led to spiritual experiences which fundamentally contradict those of the others.[40] Because of this each individual will be so locked up in, and preoccupied with, himself in a soul-spiritual sense—one could even say incarcerated—that unless through his own moral efforts he turns to Christ he will of necessity seek the solution of his growing problems in the incarnated Ahriman as mankind's greatest benefactor. Ahriman will, however, lead such people—who will have already become his clairvoyant pupils—to the ahrimanic Sorat being in the spiritual world and, hence, infinitely increase the power of this demon over people's souls. This will be a further aspect of what Rudolf Steiner means by the cosmic kamaloka which is already arriving on the Earth.

At this point some aspects of these events in the near future will be recounted in Rudolf Steiner's words. He reports: 'Ahriman would [when he incarnates] through certain stupendous arts bring to people all the clairvoyant knowledge of the kind spoken of here [in anthroposophy] which until then can be acquired only with great labour and effort [on an appropriate path of schooling]. Just think how infinitely comfortable that would be! People would not need to do anything. They would be able to live on as materialists ... and there would be no need for any spiritual efforts' (GA 191, 15 November 1919). And then Rudolf Steiner describes how Ahriman will actually achieve this: 'When Ahriman incarnates in the West at the appointed time, he would establish a great occult school; in this occult school magic arts of the most stupendous kind will be practised, and what can otherwise be acquired only with effort will be made abundantly available to mankind ... For by means of these stupendous magic arts he would be able to make great numbers of people into seers' (ibid.). But in this situation 'the worst possible advice that one could give people would be to say: "Stay just as you are! Ahriman will make all of you clairvoyant if you so desire. And you *will* desire it, because Ahriman's power will be very great!"' (ibid.).

However, the consequence of this abundant outpouring of clairvoyance will be anything but a means of furthering human progress. For ahrimanic demons will be involved in this school of magic, causing human beings to be possessed by them. This will lead to the following scenario: 'He [Ahriman] would indeed make great numbers of people into seers, but in such a way that the very considerable clairvoyant faculties of each individual would be strictly differentiated. What one person would see, a second and a third would not see. Confusion would prevail, and in spite of being made receptive to clairvoyant wisdom, people would inevitably fall into strife and discord because of the sheer diversity of their visions. Ultimately, however, they would all be very satisfied with their visions, for each of them would be able to see into the spiritual world. But the consequence of this would be that all earthly culture would fall prey to Ahriman!' (Ibid.)

In this way Ahriman, as already said, will bring about the total disintegration of humanity, a state of affairs which will then represent a very strong bulwark against what mankind needs to accomplish in the context of the sixth cultural epoch. Rudolf Steiner gives the following account of this sixth epoch, against which—since it holds the key to the entire further evolution of the Earth—the Sorat demons will campaign with particular zeal: 'That will be a time when people will possess a common wisdom to a far greater extent than at present; they will be, so to speak, immersed in a common wisdom. This will be the beginning of the feeling that the most distinctively individual aspect of a person is at the same time the most universal ... That is the guarantee for true peace and true brotherliness [amongst human individuals], because there is but *one* truth, and this truth has indeed something to do with the spiritual Sun.' (GA 103, 30 May 1908–I; italics Rudolf Steiner.)

The etherically perceptible Christ will then be active amongst mankind as the 'spiritual Sun'[41] and transform mankind into one great human community which, imbued with peace and brotherliness, will gradually become His supersensible body. Ahriman seeks already in our time to establish an opposition above all to this future by bringing about the total disintegration of mankind through his 'magic arts'. Were this to happen, what Rudolf Steiner describes in these words would come about: 'But the result would be the establishment of Ahriman's kingdom on Earth to the extent that the whole Earth falls into his grasp, and the end of everything hitherto achieved by human culture' (GA 191, 15 November 1919).

The false clairvoyance would have as its primal aim the luring of human beings into failing to perceive Christ in the etheric realm. For the ahrimanic demons will show them everything they can in the spiritual world, though not what is most important for our time; and only this can, as the 'spiritual Sun', unite the whole of humanity against everything that divides it.

Thus in our time, at whose beginning we stand today (for the first signs of ahrimanic clairvoyance are already evident in many areas), the weighty decision between the Christian and the ahrimanic clairvoyance, that is, between the Christian wisdom that unites all people or the ahrimanic that separates everyone from one another, will be made. Anthroposophy, as an orientating power for human individuals, will have an increasingly important part to play in this decision. Rudolf Steiner refers to this in the following words: 'This wisdom of the future, which is of a clairvoyant nature, must be rescued from the clutches of Ahriman. One could say that there is only *one* book, not two kinds of wisdom—*one* book. The issue is whether Ahriman has this book or Christ. Christ cannot have it unless people fight for this. And they can only fight for this by telling themselves that they must have mastered the content of spiritual science by their own efforts before the time of Ahriman's appearance on Earth.' (Ibid.; italics Rudolf Steiner.)

With this in mind he concludes by referring to the significance of anthroposophy in the present: 'You see, *that is the cosmic task of spiritual science*. It consists in preventing knowledge from becoming—and remaining—ahrimanic.' (Ibid.)

Only through a real, spiritually appropriate knowledge of evil and its influence in the world, as anthroposophy makes possible, and a conscious devotion to the power of Michael-Christ in the present time will the necessary strength and inner certainty be given to human beings to withstand the coming temptations and trials. Recognizing and over-coming all the seductive arts of Ahriman will depend existentially on whether people take up the modern path of spiritual cognition and are able to act in accordance with it. To this end, however, anthroposophists must make their contribution to proclaiming the knowledge about the etheric Christ and making it widely known; for herein lies the most important task of anthroposophy in the modern world.

The following words of Rudolf Steiner, which refer directly to our time and the immediate future, are therefore a fitting conclusion to this chapter: 'As people who understand these things and know how to interpret the signs of the times, let us order our lives in accordance with these three mysteries of our time: the mystery of Michael, the mystery of Christ and the mystery of Sorat. If we do this, we shall [be able] to work in the right way in the realm where our karma has led us.' (GA 346, 12 September 1924.)

Extract from Dostoyevsky's novel Crime and Punishment,
Raskolnikov's vision

Raskolnikov lay ill in hospital during the latter part of Lent and Eastertide. As he recovered his health, he called to mind the dreams he had had while he was feverish and delirious. He dreamt in his illness that the whole world was condemned to a terrible, hitherto unknown and unprecedented plague descending upon Europe from the depths of Asia. All were to perish except a very small number of chosen people. New kinds of parasites [trichinae] appeared, microscopic creatures that made their home in the bodies of human beings. But these creatures were endowed with intelligence and will. People who were affected by them immediately went into a frenzy and became mad. But those who were thus afflicted had never ever regarded themselves to be so intelligent and so totally possessed of the truth; never had they been more convinced of the infallibility of their judgements, their scientific conclusions, their moral convictions and beliefs. Whole villages, whole towns and nations were infected and were driven mad. All were full of anxiety and did not understand one another; each person thought that the truth resided in him alone and was in a state of torment when looking at others, beat his breast, wept and wrung his hands. They did not know whom—and how—to judge, they were unable to agree what constitutes evil and what good; they did not know whom to blame, whom to justify. People killed one another in some kind of senseless anger. They confronted one another in whole armies, but even while the armies were on the march they suddenly began to tear each other to pieces, the ranks broke up, the soldiers set about one another, stabbing and cutting, biting and devouring each other. In the towns the alarm bell was ringing all day long; everyone was being summoned, but no one knew who was summoning them or why, and everyone was in a state of alarm. The most ordinary trades were abandoned, because each person proposed his own ideas, his own improvements, and it was impossible to find agreement; and agriculture, too, was abandoned. Here and there people gathered in crowds, agreed on something together and swore a common allegiance—but then immediately started something completely different from what they had proposed, began blaming one another, fought and killed each other. There were conflagrations and famine. All people and all things were involved in destruction. The plague continued to rage and spread further. Only a few people in the whole world could be saved; they were those pure and elect individuals who were destined to found a new race of people and a new life, to renew and purify the Earth; but no one ever saw these people, no one heard their words and voices.

(Translated from the original Russian)

7. The Supersensible Mystery of Golgotha and Rudolf Steiner's Initiation

On the basis of what has been said in this book (and above all in its first chapter), there arises the question concerning the person who has brought all this knowledge to mankind in our time, namely Rudolf Steiner. As we have seen, preparing for and proclaiming the etheric Christ has been and continues to be an essential part of his mission on the Earth. One can, therefore, with justice ask why this task was placed upon Rudolf Steiner at the beginning of the twentieth century by the powers guiding the world.

In order to find an answer to this question, a further—and perhaps the most important—aspect of the etheric Second Coming needs to be included in what has been presented hitherto, an aspect to which Rudolf Steiner referred in the greatest detail on 2 May 1913 in London[1] and repeatedly returned to in later years. This has to do with the fact that the appearance of the etheric Christ in the twentieth century was preceded by a kind of repetition of the Mystery of Golgotha in the spiritual world bordering upon the Earth. The time in which this event took place coincides with the great battle that Michael had to wage between 1841 and 1879 against the spirits of darkness (see chapter 5).

In the London lecture Rudolf Steiner first speaks of how since the sixteenth century, when the materialistic and agnostic world-conception began increasingly to spread from the 'triumph of natural science' which was making itself felt everywhere, a trend which still further intensified over the ensuing centuries, an ever larger number of souls imbued with this world-conception entered the spiritual world after their death. There they spread a darkness of corresponding strength, so that a 'black sphere of materialism' arose around the Earth (GA 152). The Christ Being accordingly united with it so as to transform it from within, in order that the evolution of humanity might go forward. It was not the whole of the Christ Being that took part in this but only that aspect of His consciousness that was connected with the world of the Angels, which is closest to the Earth. The result of this was that an angelic being, through whom Christ has been active in this spiritual sphere since the Mystery of Golgotha, had to undergo a kind of death 'in the course of the nineteenth century', in order thereafter in the twentieth century to resurrect in the souls of human beings as the new Christ consciousness on Earth. Through this Christ consciousness human individuals are connected ever more deeply with the mystery of the onward striving, living Christ. Its first moment of illumination will bring about the possibility within man to encounter Christ in the etheric and subsequently to perceive Him in His two still higher revelations. Moreover, a wholly new relationship to the Mystery of Golgotha will arise amongst human beings from this Christ consciousness. They will increasingly encounter the supersensible essence of this mystery in the spirit and gain a wholly personal assurance of what actually took place at the Turning Point of Time.

Rudolf Steiner describes this second, supersensible Mystery of Golgotha in the lecture referred to in the following words: ' "The seeds of earthly materialism", which souls passing through the portals of death have borne aloft into the spiritual world in ever greater measure since the sixteenth century, causing more and more darkness, formed the "black sphere of materialism". This black sphere was, in the sense of the Manichaean principle, taken up by Christ into His Being in order to transform it, bringing about a "spiritual death by suffocation" in the angelic being in whom the Christ Being has manifested Himself since the Mystery of Golgotha. This sacrifice by Christ in the nineteenth century is comparable to the sacrifice on the physical plane in the Mystery of Golgotha and can be regarded as Christ's second crucifixion on the etheric plane. This spiritual death by suffocation which accompanied the loss of consciousness on the part of that angelic being is a repetition of the Mystery of Golgotha in the worlds lying directly behind our own, so that a reawakening of the previously hidden Christ consciousness can take place in the souls of human individuals on Earth. This reawakening is becoming the clairvoyant perception of humanity in the twentieth century ... that is, the life of Christ will from the twentieth century onwards be increasingly felt as a direct, personal experience in people's souls.'

If one has this description before one and, in the light of it, considers the biography of Rudolf Steiner in the last quarter of the nineteenth century, one can make the astonishing discovery that, in his inner path of development on the human level, he accomplished what Christ was undergoing on the cosmic level in the sphere of the Angels at almost the same time. In order to understand this decisive element of Rudolf Steiner's path of initiation somewhat better we must look more precisely at what was to be the fulfilment of his life's central task: the founding of spiritual science with its strictly scientific method of researching the spiritual worlds, which became possible only on the path of the transformation and complete spiritualization of human thinking.

To this end we must consider two basic things in Rudolf Steiner's life from his early childhood onwards. In his seventh year he discovered that he had the faculty of being able to behold the spiritual world; and a year later his first encounter with science took place at school through geometry. What was unique about Rudolf Steiner's life was that soon afterwards he resolved out of his own initiative and as though out of a hidden insight into his future mission to bring these two streams in his life consciously into connection with one another.

In his autobiography *The Course of My Life* he records this turning point in his life with the following words: 'It was in my relationship to geometry that I must perceive the first sprouting of a conception which gradually evolved within me ... Of course, I did not as a child say this to myself distinctly, but I felt that one must assimilate knowledge of the spiritual world in the same way as geometry; for the reality of the spiritual world was to me as certain as that of the world of the senses ... I had two mental images which were, to be sure, undefined but which played a considerable part in my inner life even before my eighth year. I distinguished things and beings which "are seen" and those which are "not seen"' (GA 28, chapter I). How these two worlds can be related to, and connected with, one another was henceforth to be the central spiritual task in Rudolf Steiner's life.[2]

After this fundamental experience Rudolf Steiner continued to follow both paths with all the powers at his disposal throughout his time in the upper school and until his four-year period of study at the Technical College in Vienna: the development of his supersensible faculties and assimilation of modern science in a measure and with an intensity probably possible for him alone. (At college he studied virtually all the scientific subjects offered there.[3]) And the more Rudolf Steiner progressed in this twofold direction, the more acute and decisive for his life became the question as to how these two paths can be connected with one another.

His meeting with the anonymous Master of esoteric Christianity made the corresponding spiritual instrument available to him around the time of his first Moon node independently to reach the goal that he had set before his soul. One may well imagine that Rudolf Steiner was given something through the Master's oral instruction that corresponded to the indications which can later, in a manner intended for the public eye, be found in the book *Knowledge of the Higher Worlds* (GA 10).[4] In other words, through his spiritual teacher he was introduced to the modern way of acquiring knowledge of the higher worlds, as he subsequently presented it in the book referred to. It is of decisive significance that nothing was declared to Rudolf Steiner through this personal instruction regarding the inner exertions and overall effort of the spiritual path that he was to follow. In the words that Rudolf Steiner expressed to Edouard Schuré in September 1907, the Master said something along these lines after they had been together for a short while: 'I have shown you who you are; now go and continue to be yourself!'[5] That is to say, after Rudolf Steiner had received the inner instrument for implementing his own aim, he had to follow the path leading to its fulfilment in complete solitude, in order to arrive at its culmination out of his own forces.

Now, after this mysterious encounter with the Master, Rudolf Steiner's actual work on the inner unification of the two paths began. Only at the end of his life, albeit in an objective manner that transcended the purely personal, did he convey to his anthroposophical listeners what is meant by this. Thus in the lecture of 13 January 1924 he reports for the first time how he had come to research into world evolution, the description of which forms the main chapter of his book *Occult Science* and, all in all, the heart of anthroposophy.[6] He says in this lecture: 'If you are touched by the Rosicrucian principle of initiation as understood among us here, study the system of Haeckel with all its materialism; study it, and at the same time allow yourselves to be imbued with the methods of cognition indicated in *Knowledge of the Higher Worlds*. What you learn, in a way that may be repugnant to you, about our human ancestors in Haeckel's *Anthrogenesis* needs nonetheless to be learnt in this form; for if you learn all that can be learnt about it through studying ordinary natural science and then bring this to the Gods, you will get what is related about evolution in my book *Occult Science*.' (GA 233a.)

Rudolf Steiner was indeed not the first to engage in this process; but he introduced into the whole story of evolution something that in Christian occultism was entirely new. The leading initiates of the Rosicrucian stream had already used the same method—albeit not with the science of Haeckel and Darwin but with that of Copernicus and Galileo—and achieved a great variety of things. 'The Copernican cosmology, for example, was taught in Rosicrucian schools; but in special states of consciousness the ideas contained in it came back in the way that I have explained to you here in the course of these days. Thus it was specifically Rosicrucians who realized that what people receive through modern knowledge must first be, so to speak, offered to the Gods, so that they may translate it into their own language and give it back to human beings.' (Ibid.) And then he adds: 'This possibility has remained up to the present time.'

It follows from this that the path which led to the founding of anthroposophy on the Earth can be found among Rosicrucians, one of whom—perhaps even their leader—introduced the young Rudolf Steiner to *this* method of spiritual research, to collaborating with the Gods. The proof of this can be found in Rudolf Steiner's autobiographical lecture, where he indicates how from the considerations that his Master placed before him 'things emerged in which the seeds for *Occult Science* could be sought, the book which the man that the child became later wrote'.[7]

In the same lecture from 1924 Rudolf Steiner goes on to speak of a decisive difference that existed between the early Rosicrucians and himself as regards the implementing of the same inner process, namely taking the results of modern science into one's own soul, spiritually transforming them and bringing them to the Gods. For the most advanced Rosicrucians, even Christian Rosenkreutz himself, were only able to accomplish this process through 'other dim, subconscious and sleeplike states of consciousness being called into play, conditions in which people are normally outside their body' (ibid.).

In contrast to this, Rudolf Steiner was now *the first* who carried out this whole process in full consciousness and in the body. Because he was able to do this, he was also the first Rosicrucian to be allowed to meet Michael *in full consciousness* in the spiritual world. For although—as he describes at some length in the same lecture—all true Rosicrucians constantly aspired to encounter Michael in the spiritual world, they were only able to do so in a semi-conscious or dreamlike state.[8] Only after the beginning of his current epoch of activity amongst mankind, when in 1879 he had finally cast the spirits of darkness down to the Earth from the spiritual world bordering upon it, did such an encounter with him become possible for human beings. To this end, however, Rudolf Steiner had not only to bring contemporary materialistic science to the Gods in the manner described but also naturalistic art[9] and a religion whose influence worked in the same direction.[10]

He himself describes this new way of spiritually encountering Michael in the following words: 'And as one carries up into a spiritual world the knowledge of the natural world acquired here [on the Earth] or also the creations of a naturalistic art, or again the feelings that we develop out of a religion that works naturalistically in the soul (for even religion has become naturalistic nowadays),[11] as one carries *all this* up into the spiritual world, one does indeed—granted the development of the necessary faculties—encounter Michael. Thus one may say: the old Rosicrucian movement is characterized by the fact that its most enlightened spirits had an intense longing to meet Michael; but they could do so only in a dreamlike state./Since the end of the last third of the nineteenth century human individuals have been able to meet Michael in the spirit in a fully conscious way.' (Ibid.) ∜

As we have already seen, Rudolf Steiner was the first to be able to do this. At the end of his life he described this process in the lecture of 12 August 1924 (GA 240), as though casting his eye back to his first encounter with Michael in the spiritual world bordering upon the Earth. It is worth noting that this happened around his thirty-third year, when he was working on the *Philosophy of Freedom* in Weimar. Hence the esoteric, Michaelic antecedents of this book can only really be understood from the spiritual perspective presented here.[12]

All in all one can say: before the turn of the century Rudolf Steiner took the whole scientific knowledge of his time into himself and transformed it in accordance with the inner, Rosicrucian method which he had learnt from his occult teacher, so that it could be offered up to the Gods in the spiritual world. On this path he encountered Michael and received from his cosmic sphere the impulse for his *Philosophy of Freedom*. In this sense Rudolf Steiner would write at the end of his life: 'But it may be said that the *Philosophy of Freedom* prepares the way for an understanding of the freedom which can then be experienced through a spiritual connection with Michael.'[13] Only because Rudolf Steiner himself found the path to Michael and then from him to the writing of *The Philosophy of Freedom* can this book form for its readers the bridge to Michael's present activity in the spiritual world, of which Rudolf Steiner says in the same year that 'Michael wants to be the spiritual hero of freedom' (GA 233a, 13 January 1924).

Moreover, it was the encounter with Michael in the spiritual world bordering upon the Earth that posed to Rudolf Steiner questions regarding the future of the intelligence—now become earthly but Michaelic in origin—which had already to a considerable extent been taken captive by Ahriman pre-eminently in the domain of contemporary natural science through its one-sidedly materialistic orientation, together with the whole weight of its significance for the further evolution of humanity on the Earth. He subsequently recalled this crucial experience: 'But there behind the scenes, behind this thin veil [which separates the physical from the spiritual world], in the region of Michael, great life-questions were raised' (GA 240, 12 August 1924). And he continues: 'The questions that were a living reality in the region of Michael in the 1880s and 1890s continued to have an influence when they took hold of a human individual, they worked on into the twentieth century' (ibid.).

Through this experience the question of the further destiny of the Michaelic intelligence on the Earth stood before Rudolf Steiner's inner perception, now associated with his essential task: freeing the Michaelic intelligence which had been monopolized to a considerable degree by

Ahriman in natural science and enabling it to find its way back into the spiritual domain of Michael through the free cognitive deeds of human beings. It was this that was to be Rudolf Steiner's mighty inaugurative deed around the turn of the century.

Thus Rudolf Steiner's inner path of development proceeded in three large steps: from his meeting with the Rosicrucian Master around his nineteenth year[14] to his supersensible perceiving of Michael around his thirty-third year, and finally to his decisive encounter with Christ Himself at the end of the nineteenth century.

In order to understand better how this last and highest encounter in Rudolf Steeiner's life came about, one must again recall what was said at the beginning of this chapter about the supersensible Mystery of Golgotha in the realm of the Angels. For what led to it had a similar character to what Rudolf Steiner himself inwardly underwent. Just as Christ in the macrocosm had united Himself with the 'black sphere' of materialism and inhaled its substance into Himself as a spiritual poison, so did Rudolf Steiner accomplish this on a microcosmic scale, that is, on a human level, by taking into himself in a Rosicrucian sense the whole of contemporary materialistic science, art and religion. As in the cosmos 'this black sphere [of materialism] was, in the sense of the Manichaean principle, taken by Christ into His Being in order to transform it' (GA 152, 2 May 1913), so did this happen on the Earth in the life of Rudolf Steiner who, 'in the sense of the Manichaean principle', accomplished something similar, though on the human level.[15]

As, however, the supersensible Mystery of Golgotha had already taken place and the new Christ consciousness had now been born, Rudolf Steiner was able to form a direct connection with this in the spiritual world and kindle this new Christ consciousness within his ego. But first he had to withstand the greatest trial of his life, which was associated with the spiritual path on which he had now embarked. For taking materialistic science, art and religion into his own soul signified a real and dangerous conflict with the spiritual powers which call forth this spirit-denying, materialistic tendency in present-day civilization and cause its influence to prevail within it. This conflict signified that Rudolf Steiner had to descend on the path of his initiation now in full consciousness into the sphere of the ahrimanic spirits as the true inspirers of materialistic or naturalistic science, art and religion, in order from there to raise a thinking that has become one-sidedly materialistic into the light sphere of the spirit. Whereas art and religion were also clearly implicated, the 'inner struggle against the demonic powers' (GA 28, ch. XXVI), whom Rudolf Steiner subsequently called ahrimanic beings, was nevertheless primarily concentrated against materialistic science. For the ahrimanic powers had taken possession of human thinking (which had formerly been underpinned by the Michaelic intelligence now fallen to the Earth) most strongly in this realm, so that its deliverance clearly had to begin here.

Hence at this time of his life Rudolf Steiner saw himself placed before the task of conclusively uniting both lines of his own development in one higher, indivisible unity: scientific thinking and the contemplation of the spiritual world. 'I saw in the thinking that can emerge from knowledge of nature—but at that time did not do so—the foundation on which human beings could gain insight into the spirit-world. Thus I sharply emphasized knowledge of what underlies nature, which must lead to knowledge of the spirit.' (Ibid.) For only on this path can strictly scientific thinking be borne aloft into the spiritual world, in order there as spiritual science to enable the beholding and studying of the spiritual world to become as precise, penetrated and comprehensible as can otherwise be experienced only with mathematical truths.

Already as a 22-year-old Rudolf Steiner had climbed the first steps of this path. Thus he reports at the end of his life: 'A spiritual vision confronted my soul which did not rest upon obscure mystical feelings. It came into being more through a spiritual activity which, in its transparency, might wholly be compared with mathematical thinking. I was approaching a state of mind in which I found I could believe that the perception of the spiritual world which I bore within me was justified also before the forum of scientific thinking.' (GA 28, ch. III.)

However, Rudolf Steiner still had a long path ahead of him before he could finally reach this goal. For in order to do so he had above all to imbue this spiritual consciousness that he had developed fully and wholly with the Christ impulse, in order to kindle the new Christ consciousness within himself as a consequence of the supersensible Mystery of Golgotha. This he could do only in the sphere of the ahrimanic spirits which inwardly made their presence felt at the end of the century, as he himself describes in the most important chapter of his autobiography, *The Course of My Life*. There he reports of this time: 'So much the more conscious was my inner struggle against ahrimanic powers who wanted to derive from knowledge of nature not spiritual perception but a mechanistically materialistic way of thinking' (GA 28, ch. XXVI). And then he adds: 'In my own ideas I never for one moment became a victim of this world' (ibid.).

That Rudolf Steiner while standing at this abyss could accomplish a total transformation of scientific thinking, so as to offer it up to the Gods and from them subsequently to receive anthroposophy in the form of 'spiritual science', happened only because in this ahrimanic realm he was able to kindle in his own soul the new *Christ consciousness* which had been engendered amongst mankind through the second, supersensible Mystery of Golgotha.

For this Christ consciousness, which at its first, imaginative stage can lead human beings to a perception of the etheric Christ in the spiritual world bordering upon the Earth, leads at its highest stage—of Intuition— to an experience of the inner essence of the Mystery of Golgotha itself. Thus through this meeting with Christ in Intuition Rudolf Steiner reached the culmination and at the same time the conclusion of his own initiation. He subsequently recounts this as follows: 'My soul development rested on my having stood in spirit before the Mystery of Golgotha in a most inward, most solemn festival of knowledge' (ibid.).

In the penultimate chapter of his book *An Outline of Occult Science* (1910) Rudolf Steiner presented this experience in an objective manner as the inner culmination of modern Christian-Rosicrucian initiation: 'Having thus come *through Intuition* to a knowledge of Christ in the spiritual world, the aspirant will find that he is able also to understand what took place historically on Earth in the fourth post-Atlantean period—the age of Greece and Rome' (GA 13). What is meant here is a spiritual understanding of the Mystery of Golgotha, which gives the whole of earthly evolution its meaning,[16] so that the spirit-pupil also receives full knowledge of the meaning of the Earth at this stage: 'This, then, is what the pupil of the spirit attains through Intuition: the very meaning and significance of earthly evolution are communicated to him' (ibid.).

It follows from what has been cited here that Rudolf Steiner was able to enter into a relationship to Christ and to the Mystery of Golgotha in a way that no other initiate achieved before him; for he was the first to embark on the quest for the connection of science and clairvoyance to what flowed from the supersensible Mystery of Golgotha. This happened through the developmental steps in the course of Rudolf Steiner's life which reflected the Christ event in the spiritual world and which led him to developing the highest, intuitive stage of Christ consciousness—which, in turn, he then directed towards the Mystery of Golgotha, so as at this point of world evolution to encounter Christ in Intuition, that is, from ego to ego.[17]

'After the period of probation had subjected me to arduous battles of the soul, I had to immerse myself in Christianity and, indeed, in the world in which it is illumined from a spiritual standpoint,' (GA 28, XXVI) wrote Rudolf Steiner in his autobiography. Through this he arrived at the deepest knowledge of the great Mystery of Golgotha at the Turning Point of Time from a purely spiritual perspective, that is, from the new Christ consciousness engendered in the nineteenth century through the supersensible Mystery of Golgotha and whose first dissemination amongst mankind in the twentieth century led to the beholding of Christ in the etheric.

One can also say that Rudolf Steiner beheld the first Mystery of Golgotha with the consciousness of the second Mystery of Golgotha and, through this, came to the spiritual content of anthroposophical Christology, culminating in what he imparted from the domain of the Fifth Gospel (GA 148). From this it becomes understandable that Rudolf Steiner spoke in one and the same year (1913) on the one hand for the first time about the supersensible Mystery of Golgotha and, on the other, about the Fifth Gospel, for from a spiritual point of view they belong inseparably together. *For only a Christ consciousness that has been kindled in the human ego by the second Mystery of Golgotha has the capacity to behold the events of the Turning Point of Time and communicate them to human beings in the way that Rudolf Steiner did in his lectures on the Fifth Gospel.*

In the following words written at the end of his life Rudolf Steiner indicated that this new path to Christ must first lead through the cosmic sphere of Ahriman with all its associated trials and dangers, where only the full power of the Christ consciousness—as a light in the darkness—can light a flame: 'But Christ will be there; through His great sacrifice He will live in the same sphere in which Ahriman also lives. Man will be able to choose between Christ and Ahriman.'[18]

This is a clear characterization of the modern *Michaelic* path to Christ which Rudolf Steiner himself followed at the end of the nineteenth century and which he subsequently described in the 26th chapter of his autobiography, without mentioning the name of the Time Spirit. Somewhat later, however, in October 1924, he defined this path in the following words: 'Such people see how—*through the image of Michael* in Ahriman's sphere—man is to be led in freedom away from Ahriman to Christ.'[19] The 'image of Michael' is to be taken as meaning not only the memory of the supersensible encounter with him in the 1880s and 1890s but also his reflection which every person today brings with him from out of the time before birth in his etheric body and bears within himself in earthly life. (The origin and nature of this reflection have already been described in the fifth chapter of this book.) Rudolf Steiner's own words must be appended here, words which in this connection have a special, autobiographical character; for they describe how he himself experienced this reflection of Michael in his own etheric body and confirm that it remained with him as a unique guiding influence in the fulfilment of his difficult task: 'But then, behind the human being, as it were—for people see higher things with the back of the head—the outer cosmic form of Michael, towering, radiant, retaining his cosmic nature but reflecting it in the person's higher nature, so that the human individual presents an *etheric reflection* of the cosmic figure of Michael' (GA 223, 27 September 1923).

It is doubtless the case that at this time it was Rudolf Steiner himself who bore the reflection of Michael most strongly within his own being; for although each person is furnished with this on the path to an earthly incarnation, Rudolf Steiner was because of his encounter—as described earlier—with the Time Spirit in the spiritual world bordering upon the Earth able to strengthen it to a considerable degree. In this way he was, moreover, now well equipped to accomplish the hardest part of his task.

Thus after his encounter with Michael in the time when he had researched and described the nature of human freedom in its full ramifications in his principal early work, Rudolf Steiner had the task of descending in the years that followed into the ahrimanic sphere with the reflection of Michael in his own etheric body in order to discover the sources of materialistic science, and of thereby transforming it into modern spiritual science, so that in it—or to be more precise from it—the new path to Christ could be found.[20]

In another context Rudolf Steiner refers in the following words to the experience which was also *his own experience* at the end of the nineteenth century and which signified this dangerous step on his path and at the same time the culmination of his initiation: 'We are here pointing to the abyss of nothingness in human evolution which man must cross when he becomes a free being. It is the influence of Michael together with the Christ impulse that makes this leap possible.'[21]

In these words this leap across the abyss of nothingness is described more from an objective, cosmic aspect. When viewed from the standpoint of modern initiation, what is going on here is man's inner encounter with his true ego and at the same time with Christ, who makes it possible for every human being to experience the true ego. Thus one can say: Michael in our time leads the spirit-pupil to the abyss of existence, where he must experience himself as absolute nothingness in the face of complete nothingness. The pupil of the spirit has to cross this abyss by using all the inner strength and trustfulness of which his soul is capable, in order on the other side to receive his true ego. Rudolf Steiner describes this decisive experience on the path of modern initiation in the following words: 'But one stands wholly rightly and in a true manner at the abyss of existence if one forms the resolve to extinguish or forget oneself through one's free inner volition, through an energetic act of will . . . to dwell for a while in the spiritual world at the abyss of existence in confronting nothingness as nothing. It is the most shattering experience that one can have, and one must pass through this experience with great trustfulness. In order as nothingness to traverse the abyss it is necessary that one has the trust that the true ego *is brought to meet* one from the world. And this is what happens . . . Thus the ascent to the super-spiritual world is an inner experience, the experience of a completely new world at the abyss of existence and *the receiving* of the true ego from this super-spiritual world at the abyss of existence.' (GA 147, 30 August 1913.)

And if on the basis of this description we now ask ourselves *who* 'brings' the true ego 'to meet us' from the higher spiritual world in which we stand after crossing the abyss and which is here referred to as a 'super-spiritual world', and from *whom* may we—once we have withstood this greatest trial of modern initiation—'receive' our own true ego, our true human essence, the answer is completely clear: *from Christ Himself,* who as the divine 'I am' in the macrocosm occupies the same central position as does this true ego in the microcosm of the human individual. 'Christ gives me my humanity'[22]—here, once he has been enabled to receive his true ego from the hands of Christ on yonder side of the cosmic abyss, the human individual experiences the highest form of Christ consciousness lighting up within him, the intuitive merging of the human 'I' with the 'I' of Christ. Henceforth he bears in his ego the reflection of Christ's Ego, without having in the least degree to forfeit his own individuality as an ego.

Michael is in our time leading people to this initiation at the abyss of existence; and Christ Himself receives the person who is being initiated at the other side, in order that through this new Christ consciousness in his true ego He might remain inseparably united with him. This is the path whereby in our time Michael and Christ make it possible for a human individual to take hold of his true ego.

That a person encounters Christ on yonder shore of world existence is the direct consequence of the supersensible Mystery of Golgotha. It is true that the possibility for this was created already at the Turning Point of Time with the great Mystery of Golgotha, but only after its repetition in the supersensible world was the *conscious* receiving of the true ego possible. What for mankind as a whole will be the awakening of Christ consciousness, leading to the beholding of the etheric Christ,[23] is for the initiate the experience of his true ego, which he receives at the abyss of existence from the hands of Christ, who has passed through the second, supersensible Mystery of Golgotha.[24]

Rudolf Steiner spoke about this supersensible Mystery of Golgotha for the first time on 8 February 1913 in Berlin at an instruction lesson for the cultic section of his Esoteric School: 'What is new and what will now gradually be revealed to human beings is a recollection or repetition of what St Paul experienced at Damascus. He beheld the etheric body of Christ. The reason why this will now become visible to us derives from the fact that what could be called a new Mystery of Golgotha has taken place in the etheric world. What took place here in the physical world at the Crucifixion as a result of the hatred of uncomprehending humanity has now been repeated on the etheric level owing to the hatred of human beings who have entered the etheric world as materialists after death.' (GA 265.)[25]

And then in the same instruction lesson Rudolf Steiner connects the supersensible Mystery of Golgotha with the central sign of the Rosicrucians: with the black cross surrounded by seven red roses. Whereas in earlier Rosicrucianism this sign signified a reference to the Mystery of Golgotha at the Turning Point of Time (which is why the middle part of the Rosicrucian dicta had the words 'In *Jesu* morimur',[26] because the old Rosicrucians primarily beheld Christ's death in Jesus), in the new Rosicrucianism of anthroposophy[27] the sign of the cross with the seven roses has become the symbol of the second, supersensible Mystery of Golgotha, which is why Rudolf Steiner changed the middle part of the Rosicrucian dicta into 'In *Christo* morimur'.

Rudolf Steiner also spoke as follows about this new connection: 'Let us visualize once more how, at the Mystery of Golgotha, a cross of dead wood was erected on which the body of Christ hung. And then let us visualize the wood of that cross in the etheric world as green, sprouting and living wood which has been turned to charcoal by the flames of hatred and on which only seven blossoming roses appear, representing Christ's sevenfold nature.[28] There we have the picture of the second Mystery of Golgotha which has now taken place in the etheric world. And through this dying, this second death of Christ, we have gained the possibility of beholding that etheric body [in which the etheric Christ appears to human beings].' (Ibid.)

If at this point one bears in mind that the founder of the Rosicrucian stream, Christian Rosenkreutz, was himself 'present at the Mystery of Golgotha'[29] and was, therefore, the decisive witness of 'how, at the Mystery of Golgotha, a cross of dead wood was erected on which the body of Christ hung', and adds that Rudolf Steiner became in the spirit just as great a witness of the second, supersensible Mystery of Golgotha,[30] one will understand the full significance of the imagination that he communicated to Ita Wegman in 1924 through a personal conversation. Following on from the meditation that he had given her, beginning with the lines:

Ich halte die Sonne in mir
Er[31] führt als König mich in die Welt

(I hold the Sun within me
As King he leads me into the world)

he went on to say: 'One should think of oneself in a white garment, walking towards the altar, before which Christian Rosenkreutz stands on the left with a blue stole and Rudolf Steiner on the right with a red stole. One must think of this altar as being in the spiritual world.' And then Ita Wegman adds that 'on another occasion Rudolf Steiner said that in the

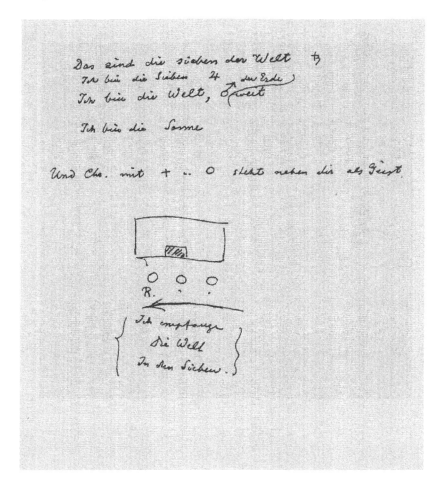

spiritual world the figures wearing these stoles stand side by side'.[32] At the end of the meditation Rudolf Steiner added a further sentence after the last line 'Ich bin die Sonne' (I am the Sun):

Und Chr. mit + ... o steht neben dir als Geist (ibid.)
(And Chr. with + ... o stands as spirit beside you).

And by way of an explanation he drew for Ita Wegman the spiritual altar before which Christ reveals Himself (in many of the meditations that he gave, Rudolf Steiner abbreviated the name 'Christ' with the letters 'Chr.'), and before which Christian Rosenkreutz and Rudolf Steiner stand, receiving the pupil of the spirit as he approaches the altar. (Christian Rosenkreutz is identified with the letter 'R' to the left of the spirit-pupil.[33])

It becomes apparent from this context that the sign in the additional line of the meditation (+ ... o) can mean not only the cross and the roses but also, in the sense of the drawing referred to and its explanation, Christian Rosenkreutz (+) and Rudolf Steiner (o) standing at Christ's altar.

These two forms together form the sign with which Rudolf Steiner concluded the Christmas Conference after the words from the Foundation Stone Meditation[34]

O Light Divine,
O Sun of Christ,
Warm Thou
Our Hearts,
Enlighten Thou
Our Heads!

(GA 260, 1 January 1924)

Here the cross relates to the light that enlightens heads, and the circle to the warmth that overwhelms and fills hearts; but at the same time they also signify Christian Rosenkreutz and Rudolf Steiner standing before the spiritual altar.[35] For *these* Masters are the representatives for our time of the two most important deeds of the Christ Being: the Mystery of Golgotha at the Turning Point of Time and the second in our time in the spiritual world.

Rudolf Steiner also described the altar before which the two Masters stand *after* the Christmas Conference, during the third meeting of the so-called 'Wachsmuth-Lerchenfeld Group'.[36] Thus on 3 January 1924 in Dornach he said that if we really wanted to awaken in our ego, as opposed to our habitual condition of sleep, we would have to avail ourselves of the help of the following imagination: 'Altar, the Sun above it. We approach the altar and experience ourselves wholly as shadow, as completely beingless. Formerly we said: I am. Now we say consciously: I am not. A divine being then descends from the Sun above the altar and fills the shadow with life. We are like a chalice which receives the light of the divine being which descends out of the Sun—through grace we receive this divinity, it bestows itself on us.' (GA 265.)

This meeting with Christ—for the Godhead which descends out of the Sun and brings life to man's true ego and makes it conscious, so that it becomes an inner Grail chalice, can only be the Christ Himself—takes place at the supersensible sacrificial altar (the Godhead from the Sun gives Himself to us here), before which Christian Rosenkreutz and Rudolf Steiner stand today as its guardians in the spiritual world. This imagination is also indicative of the nature of the Grail mysteries in our time, which have already been spoken of in chapter 2. These mysteries have to do with the receiving of a copy of Christ's Ego into man's enlivened and trans-formed ego. The first person who was able to achieve this in the epoch of the consciousness soul was Christian Rosenkreutz. Rudolf Steiner speaks about this as follows: 'From the sixteenth century onwards, copies of Christ's Ego begin to weave themselves into the egos of particular individualities, one of them being Christian Rosenkreutz, the first Rosicrucian.' And he adds that this will have the following effect: 'it is because of this that a more intimate relationship with Christ became possible' (GA 109/111, 28 March 1909); for there can be no more intimate relationship with Christ than through receiving a copy of His Ego into one's own ego.

Rudolf Steiner achieved this stage as well, though on the path which from our time onwards must gradually become that of all people. This is the path that anthroposophy describes and which has become possible for human beings only since the beginning of the present Michael epoch (1879) and the end of Kali Yuga (1900). Hence Rudolf Steiner speaks of how in our time working intensively with anthroposophy can prepare people for this goal and lead them towards it.[37]

The same applies to Christ's appearance in the etheric. Likewise in this realm anthroposophy has something of great importance to accomplish.

In our time and in the immediate future it must proclaim the etheric Second Coming and spiritually prepare people on Earth for it. As Rudolf Steiner indicates in these three brief quotations, 'it is the obligation of anthroposophy to proclaim this'; for 'spiritual science needs to prepare mankind for this future event', and 'we disseminate anthroposophy in order to bring about a knowledge of this'.[38]

What Rudolf Steiner had to accomplish so to speak on the stage of world history amidst humanity as a whole Christian Rosenkreutz and his pupils were obliged to deal with supersensibly from an esoteric aspect. This has to do with the continuing activity of the etheric body of Christian Rosenkreutz, which has since his initiation in the thirteenth century existed in the spiritual world bordering upon the Earth. This etheric body has until the twentieth century been influential only within the esoteric schools of Rosicrucians. 'The twentieth century has the task of enabling this etheric body to become so mighty that it can also work exoterically ... Until now this etheric body has extended its influence only to the Rosicrucian school; in the twentieth century more and more people will be able to experience its effect, and through this they will come to experience Christ's appearance in the etheric body. It is the work of Rosicrucians that makes it possible for people to have an etheric vision of Christ.' (GA 130, 27 September 1911.)

Thus one can say: the work of Christian Rosenkreutz and his pupils ('with his hosts') comes forth from its esoteric background and manifests itself exoterically amongst mankind as a whole; for those people who are overshadowed by this etheric body of Christian Rosenkreutz thereby receive the faculty of beholding the etheric Christ.

Rudolf Steiner's earthly activity, in contrast, unfolded in the opposite direction. His path led from the dissemination of the modern path of initiation amongst mankind verbally and in writing through anthroposophy to the founding of the new mysteries at the Christmas Conference, with its spiritual core in the Michael School, whose Third Class was to lead directly to Christ as he works in the spiritual world at the present time.

In his book *The Foundation Stone* F.W. Zeylmans van Emmichoven referred to this mystery in the following words: 'Both Rudolf Steiner and Christian Rosenkreutz lead the Sun of Christ to us, but their ways of working—from without inwards and then out again, or from within outwards and then back to inwardness—constantly interpenetrate each other, like delicate red and blue hues, producing through this mingling the peach-blossom colour of the etheric, in which the Sun of Christ lights up for us.'[39]

This peach-blossom colour is at the same time that of the etheric Second Coming, in which the Sun of Christ shines forth for present-day humanity and at whose altar in the spiritual world Rudolf Steiner and Christian Rosenkreutz stand in our time.

One can also say that Christian Rosenkreutz, as the reincarnated Lazarus-John, passes from the inner experiences involved in the awakening of Lazarus in Bethany to standing at that crucial moment in world history as a witness beneath the Cross on Golgotha and then to his secret initiation in the thirteenth century,[40] the consequence of which was the esoteric influence of his etheric body amongst mankind.[41] Rudolf Steiner's path, on the other hand, went in the opposite direction. Beginning from the public presentation of his theory of knowledge in his early philosophical work, he became the first witness of the second, supersensible Mystery of Golgotha when, in consequence of it, he was the first to raise the new Christ consciousness to the stage of Intuition, in order on this foundation to establish anthroposophy amongst mankind in the twentieth century as a modern science of the spirit.

From what has been said the answer to the question posed at the beginning of this chapter can now be answered: why was Rudolf Steiner chosen by the world rulership for the task of preparing for Christ's etheric appearance and proclaiming this to humanity? This happened because he was the first Rosicrucian to enter into the stream of the second, supersensible Mystery of Golgotha which is itself the source of Christ's Second Coming, in order to kindle within himself the new Christ consciousness which alone validates preparing for and proclaiming the etheric Christ.

Thus Rudolf Steiner is and remains *the* great proclaimer and preparer of this event in cultural history, who as a modern Rosicrucian initiate has collaborated in our time as no one else before him in 'recognizing and realizing the intentions of the *living Christ* ... in the form of complete wisdom, beauty and activity'.[42]

★

The other mystery which is connected with the entire fifth post-Atlantean cultural epoch, but can only be fully encompassed by the consciousness of human beings through the second, supersensible Mystery of Golgotha, is that of evil. Of the seven, unspoken mysteries known to the old tradition of Christian occultism, the fifth is associated with it and relates to the present, fifth cultural epoch.[43] Rudolf Steiner expresses this in the following words: 'Now, when Christ is to appear again in the etheric, when a kind of Mystery of Golgotha is to be experienced anew, evil will have a significance similar to that of birth and death for the fourth post-Atlantean epoch ... Thus by a strange paradox the humanity of the fifth post-Atlantean period is led to a renewed experience of the Mystery of Golgotha through the forces of evil [as a result of the 'spiritual death by suffocation' which they called forth]. Through the experience of evil it will be possible for the Christ to appear again' (GA 185, 25 October 1918).

This key experience of Rudolf Steiner's spiritual research enables one to understand why, as no other initiate of modern times, he was through his unique relationship to the supersensible Mystery of Golgotha in a position to research into the abyss of evil in all its various aspects and to communicate these mysteries to human beings through anthroposophy in the light of the new Michael revelation. For also today, 85 years after his death, it needs to be said that neither before Rudolf Steiner nor after him has mankind received so extensive a revelation of the mysteries of evil as was given through anthroposophy. And the more widely people take these truths that have been imparted to them fully into their consciousness, the stronger will be the bulwark that they will be erecting against the overwhelming power of the adversaries in the world. Moreover, according to a remark made by Rudolf Steiner to Ita Wegman the possibility can be created for the higher hierarchies to be able to gain an impression from the consciousness of human beings of the demonic mysteries which they have come to recognize with the help of spiritual science; and on the foundation of this knowledge gained by humanity they can be enabled to help mankind far more effectively and in quite another way in its struggle with evil than would otherwise have been the case. Ita Wegman later recounted this conversation in the following words: 'Only human beings are able to have knowledge of the mysteries of demons. The Gods await these mysteries which people bring to them ... Through such human deeds of offering up to the Gods mysteries wrested from demons, the dark influences of these demons will be warded off; and so where darkness formerly prevailed, spiritual light can once more ray forth.'[44]

In connection with this conversation Rudolf Steiner also gave Ita Wegman a verse for meditation which demonstrates the possibility that the higher hierarchies and Michael himself have for helping human beings in their struggle with evil:

There, where the light
In face of green demons
Is tremulous,
And the primordial Powers

Born of the light
To wrestling men
Proclaim the riddle
Which from the demons
Only by men can be enticed forth
And brought to the Gods,
There soul found soul
In order to offer some day to waiting Gods
The secrets of demons
In a darkened place—
That light may be born,
Where for want of this deed
Eternal darkness held sway.
Such a place there is
It must vanish
Make it some day vanish.
So speaks the admonishing
Gaze of Michael.'[45]

Thus one can say that the mighty revelation of the mysteries of evil that pervades Rudolf Steiner's entire work is, from an esoteric standpoint, none other than the continuing influence of the spiritual impulse which has its source in the supersensible Mystery of Golgotha in the second half of the nineteenth century. And if one bears in mind that the lecture in which Rudolf Steiner speaks with particular power about the second Mystery of Golgotha had as its principal theme the new revelation of Michael since the year 1879, one begins to discern how the two beings of Michael and Christ were active in Rudolf Steiner's biography. How this occurred in actual terms is apparent from the following words of the same lecture: 'Michael can give us *new spiritual light,* which we may regard as a transformation of the light given through him at the time of the Mystery of Golgotha, and the people of our time may receive this light' (GA 152, 2 May 1913). Rudolf Steiner is referring here to the present transformation of the original Mystery of Golgotha brought about by its supersensible repetition in the spiritual world. Thus Christ is working amongst mankind today through the spirit of Michael who serves Him; and their emissary for our time is Rudolf Steiner.

Conclusion: The Second Coming and the Tasks of the Anthroposophical Society

To conclude what has been presented here on the theme of this book, I should like to emphasize two further aspects of the etheric Second Coming which can be of particular significance for the present and future development of the Anthroposophical Society; for with respect to both aspects it has an important task to fulfil at the present time.

Reference has already been made in chapter 2 to the first aspect. In the lecture of 26 December 1914 which is quoted there, Rudolf Steiner compares anthroposophy with the Christmas child and indicates that anthroposophy is called upon to be developed ever more and more by those people who are connected with it, in order that it may become a fully mature being in which the etheric Christ can incarnate.

If one bears in mind that one of the principal tasks of the Anthroposophical Society is the cultivation of anthroposophy, one can see the whole life of the Society in a new light: it has the task of becoming, through the spiritual work of its members, a bearer of the etheric Christ. As one considers the future of the Anthroposophical Society in this vast perspective, one can also draw from this the strength gradually to do justice to this task.

The second aspect, which is inseparably connected with the etheric Second Coming but goes far beyond it in temporal terms, is Christ's initial activity in our time as the Lord of Karma. Likewise in this regard, one of Rudolf Steiner's observations is of decisive significance. Whereas he connects the onset of the Second Coming with the 1930s and gives on several occasions a time-span of 3000 years for its full unfolding, he says of Christ's new karmic office that it will last until the end of Earth evolution. (See p. 12) Rudolf Steiner gives the end of the twentieth century as the beginning of Christ's activity as the Lord of karma, that is, the present time. 'Just as on the physical plane an event took place in Palestine at the beginning of our era in which Christ played the important part, an event which has significance for the whole of mankind, so in the course of the twentieth century, *towards the end of the twentieth century*, a significant event will again take place, not in the physical world but in the world we usually call the world of the etheric. This event will have as fundamental a significance for the evolution of humanity as the event of Palestine had at the beginning of our era ... This event has to do with the transferring in the twentieth century—in a more elevated form than hitherto—of a certain office in the universe associated with the evolution of mankind to the Christ. Occult, clairvoyant research teaches us that in our epoch the important event occurs that Christ is becoming the Lord of Karma for human evolution.' (GA 131, 7 October 1911.)

If one bears in mind that, when re-founding the Anthroposophical Society at the Christmas Conference, Rudolf Steiner entrusted it with the highly important task of working consciously with the ordering of karma, so that gradually a first free karmic community might arise, one can also view this task in its proper spiritual perspective and dimension.[1] Rudolf Steiner says in this regard: 'What is it that unites the members of the Anthroposophical Society? It is that they are to bring order again into their karma! . . . Then it is the case that people are striving to recover their karma, their real karma, their endeavour is to live and manifest their real karma. This is the cosmic ray that shines clearly through the anthroposophical movement, clearly perceptible to those who know: restoring the truth of karma'—but this is already in the context of Christ's new karmic office. 'In this connection we can understand much relating both to the destiny of individuals in the Anthroposophical Society and to the destiny of the whole Society' (GA 237, 8 August 1924). May the numerous past conflicts of the Anthroposophical Society, which despite their deep tragedy can nevertheless in themselves be understood as a necessary part of the whole path leading to the goal referred to, also be understood in *this* sense.[2]

In particular the whole body of karma lectures, which Rudolf Steiner had already begun to give during the Christmas Conference, can from this point of view appear to us in a new light. For they form a basis for understanding that human individuals are gradually becoming the conscious collaborators of Christ as the Lord of Karma. If at this point one also recalls that Rudolf Steiner referred to the research in this domain as his own task[3] and therefore wanted to begin with it right at the start of his anthroposophical activity, one can appreciate how deeply and centrally it was connected with the preparation for Christ's assuming of this office.

Thus it is distressing to learn subsequently from a lecture by Rudolf Steiner himself that—after the failure of the attempt already in 1902 to carry out 'practical karma exercises' within the newly founded German Section of the Theosophical Society—he then had to wait a full 21 years before he was finally able to begin with this central theme of his whole life's work at the Christmas Conference.

He himself recalls this in a karma lecture: 'But now, with more than two decades of preparatory work behind us, a beginning must be made with real esotericism.[4] The Christmas Conference, when the esoteric impulse came into the Society, could take place, and so now a link can be made with that time when the intention was to introduce this esoteric trend into the Society.' (GA 240, 16 April 1924.)

What was stopped in 1902 through people's failure to understand gave certain ahrimanic spirits the opportunity to intervene and, in an anti-Michaelic sense, deprived Rudolf Steiner of the possibility of communicating these karmic truths of the world any earlier. He also speaks about this in the karma lectures: 'Indeed, through all that happened since the Christmas Conference of the Anthroposophical Society, through the opportunities that I have been given since that time to engage in occult work—the things to which I refer are not new (even though in occultism one cannot immediately communicate things that one has discovered only the day before), they were experienced a long time ago in the way that I have indicated to you—the demons who have hitherto [before the Christmas Conference] prevented these things from being voiced have been compelled to remain silent' (GA 240, 12 August 1924).[5]

The karma lectures themselves culminate without doubt in the description of the karma of the *Anthroposophical Society*, as Rudolf Steiner referred to the theme (and not of the *anthroposophical movement*, as one might have expected him to do). These lectures are concerned with a group of people who have in their existence before birth been associated with Michael for hundreds of years and have taken part in his supersensible school and the cosmic cultus to reveal the Sun karma connecting them with Michael, in order to endow them with the inner strength to overcome their past Moon karma and, hence, together establish a new karmic community on the Earth which shall become a conscious instrument of Christ's present activity as the Lord of Karma.[6]

Now that from the end of the twentieth century Christ has fully taken over this office, the Anthroposophical Society will become worthy of the essential purpose of its re-founding at Christmas 1923 only if it seeks to embrace and implement *this* task assigned to it by Rudolf Steiner.

In the Foundation Stone Meditation, which formed the esoteric focus of the Christmas Conference and is an essential part of the foundation of the General Anthroposophical Society, there is a clear reference to both these aspects of the present Christ mystery. The Christ Being is directly addressed on two occasions in this meditation and mentioned by name. The first reference comes at the beginning of the macrocosmic section of the second part:

For the Christ Will in the encircling round holds sway
In the rhythms of the worlds, blessing the soul

(GA 260, 25 December 1923).

These words point directly to Christ's activity as the Lord of Karma, whose karma-ordering will works in the spiritual aura of the Earth and is revealed in the 'rhythms of the worlds', which also include the great journey that a human being makes through his various incarnations.[7] The threads of destiny are so interwoven by Christ on this path that the balancing out of personal karma can serve the greatest possible benefit of mankind. Thus a person learns in a new way to work freely and with good will on his karma, so that it is transformed from the law of iron necessity into a grace that he now experiences as proceeding from Christ Himself.[8]

The other aspect of Christ's present activity is referred to in the lines from the fourth part of the Foundation Stone Meditation, with which—as we have seen—Rudolf Steiner concluded the Christmas Conference:

O Light Divine,
O Sun of Christ!
Warm Thou
Our Hearts,
Enlighten Thou
Our Heads!

(ibid.)

These words are concerned with the ascent of the spiritual Sun of Christ in the souls of human individuals who have transformed their hearts and heads and are bringing them into inner harmony and concord, which is necessary for the raying forth of the new clairvoyance that leads to an experience of the etheric Christ.

Moreover, through the sequence 'heart-head' in these words there is a reference to the stream of the etherized blood of Christ within man, which through its connection with the stream of etherized human blood likewise leads to the perception of the etheric Christ. However, in order that these two streams within a human individual are able to unite, he must truly 'fire' the etherized stream of his blood with spiritual-scientific knowledge, that is, bring to it a real, heartfelt enthusiasm.

Rudolf Steiner describes this in the following words: 'But the evolution of humanity progresses; and in our present age what matters is that people should recognize the need for the knowledge contained in spiritual science and gradually bring the fire of inspiration to what streams from the heart to the brain so that it furnishes an understanding of anthroposophy. The consequence of this will be that individuals will be able to receive and comprehend the event that has its beginning in the twentieth century, which is the appearance of the etheric Christ as opposed to the physical Christ of Palestine.' (GA 130, 1 October 1911.) Herein lies the third task of the Anthroposophical Society: to be the place in the world where this is possible, where people are able so to take up anthroposophy that they fire their souls with true enthusiasm for a knowledge of the spirit appropriate to our times.

This can indeed happen if they first strongly take hold of their head forces through a thinking that is both clear and intense and then extend this thinking down to the heart, in order there to bring about the union of the two streams. It is this that can be understood as the true Michael knowledge that leads human individuals to Christ today. 'The age of Michael has dawned. Hearts are beginning to have thoughts; spiritual fervour is no longer streaming only from mystical obscurity but from a clarity of soul that is engendered by thought. If one understands this, one is receiving Michael into one's heart.'[9] And if a person achieves this, he also gains a conscious access to the sphere of the etheric Christ which is alone appropriate for the spirit of our time, for it is 'the uniting of oneself with Michael that also enables one to find one's way to Christ'.[10]

The three esoteric tasks of the Anthroposophical Society referred to here, which can be fulfilled only on the path of Michael in the service of the etheric Second Coming and in association with the Lord of Karma, show how strongly Rudolf Steiner saw the future of this Society already at its founding in connection with the most important spiritual events of our time and the beings who are involved with them—a relationship that he did all he could to forge along these lines. So may the Anthroposophical Society remain faithful to the task that it has received from Rudolf Steiner and from the spiritual world.

Appendix: The Relationship to Christ Today[1]

One of the most important results of Rudolf Steiner's spiritual-scientific research is the fact that mankind as a whole crossed the threshold of the spiritual world in the second half of the nineteenth century and, hence, has already been living on the other side of the threshold for over a century (though not the slightest notice has been taken of this). However, the actual process of crossing the threshold takes place on various levels, so that Rudolf Steiner also speaks in certain contexts of how mankind was at the beginning of the twentieth century—and will continue to be for some while—still in the midst of this process. (See GA 192, 1 May 1919.)

In other places he gives absolutely precise temporal indications. For example, he says in the following words: 'There we come to an abyss. In the 1840s this knowledge was completely lost [the connection with the old mysteries through the still extant teachings of Aristotle], and the abyss remained until the end of the century, when the coming of the Michael age brought the possibility for these truths to be found again [the link with the essence of the mysteries through anthroposophy]. When, however, people traversed this abyss, they were actually crossing a threshold. And at this threshold stands a guardian. Mankind was not at first able to see this guardian when it passed him by between the years 1842 and 1879. But now, for its own good, it must look back and take note of him. For a failure to pay heed to him and living on into the following centuries without taking notice of him would lead mankind to complete disaster.' (GA 233a, 12 January 1924.)

The need referred to here to raise this deed of having crossed the threshold into full awareness is accordingly one of the most important tasks of our time. Moreover, the situation that has been characterized can be used as a key to all manner of phenomena of the present time. For example, it offers an answer to the question why—especially after the historical experiences of the twentieth century—the forces of evil in the world are stronger than those of good. The reality is that this is by no means the case; for the good powers are from the outset immeasurably stronger than their evil counterparts. The explanation for this phenomenon is that after the crossing of the threshold spiritual beings have acquired a far more direct access to people's subconscious minds.

This reveals a fundamental difference in the working of good and evil powers. The former are characterized by the full account that they take today of human freedom and by their commitment that human beings themselves take the first step to approach them, so that they create the necessary conditions for collaboration out of their freedom and, hence, gain access to the help that they will increasingly need in the future. The forces of evil, in contrast, have absolutely no respect for human freedom. They thrust their way into people's subconscious and do all they can to seize the opportunity presented by the fact that mankind has already been living for many decades beyond the threshold and, if unaware of this, can neither recognize nor reject the adversarial powers active in this sphere.

In the book *Knowledge of the Higher Worlds: How is it achieved?*, in the chapter entitled 'Division of the Personality during Spiritual Training', Rudolf Steiner describes the basic quality of the crossing of the threshold by saying that after it has been crossed man's three soul-forces of thinking, feeling and will are loosened from the natural connection brought about in the sense-perceptible world by the physical body and threaten to—as it were—tear a person's soul-life apart in various directions. In order to withstand this trial at the threshold he needs the strengthened power of his ego to bring the three soul-forces together in a new way. Unless he recognizes the source of this divided state, one of three forces— depending on his inner disposition—will gain hold of him. Thus he can stray into 'three aberrations': he can develop a loveless, cold nature if thinking preponderates in him, or where feeling takes the upper hand he becomes someone who develops an increasingly alien relationship to the earthly world. And a person with a surfeit of will develops a commanding and violent nature that seeks exclusively to dominate other beings.

Rudolf Steiner goes on to observe in the same chapter that these three aberrations can intensify further with time. Such a person is 'for outward observation, and also from the standpoint of materialistic medicine, hardly distinguishable ... from someone who is insane or at least suffering from severe nervous illness' (GA 10).

Anthroposophy gives many indications which create a sure foundation for the spirit-pupil to avoid these aberrations. In what follows a particular path will be shown whereby the three soul-forces can be purified and held together at the threshold, namely out of the heightened and spiritualized power of the individual ego. This has to do with the possibility of filling each of the three soul-forces with the Christ impulse, in order then to draw them together in a new way out of the Christ-endowed ego.

If from this point of view we look once more at the content of the book *Knowledge of the Higher Worlds*, we find that the manifold guidance given there for developing the inner life has two fundamental aspects. On the one hand there are many different actual exercises enabling the development of new clairvoyant faculties; and, on the other, many moral capacities which the pupil must consciously cultivate in himself alongside these exercises. The former relates to the latter in accordance with the '*golden* rule of genuine occult science' (ibid., italics Rudolf Steiner) as does one to three: 'For every *one* step forward that you take in seeking knowledge of occult truths, take *three* steps forward in the improvement of your own character' (ibid., italics Rudolf Steiner). The particular importance of such moral qualities is also apparent in that in the first chapter ('Conditions') Rudolf Steiner devotes six whole pages to the significance of one of them, which he also calls an unconditional 'fundamental attitude' of the soul: veneration, devotion, reverence, which together form the so-called 'path of veneration'.

One can discern the effect of both these developmental processes in the example of the awakening of the lotus flowers. The exercises in thinking (meditation and concentration) bring about their growth and their mobility; whereas the educating of moral qualities gives them the right form and the necessary maturity. With the pupil's further development both these processes manifest themselves in a decisive way when the guardian of the threshold is encountered; the exercises themselves lead to the capacity to perceive the guardian, the moral qualities that one has newly acquired also make it possible for him to be endured. To a considerably intensified degree this is also the case with the encounter with the Greater Guardian.

Let us now consider the two processes more closely. The first consists in the pupil's active meditative life. This involves the imbuing of thinking with the impulse of will, thus also enabling a person to experience his freedom to a heightened degree. Hence Rudolf Steiner regards meditating as one of the freest of human deeds. He says in this regard: 'When a person begins to meditate, he is carrying out the only act that is truly free' (GA 214, 20 August 1922). What is involved here is wholly to transform thinking through the exertions of the will and above all to make it completely free of the body.

In this connection Rudolf Steiner describes two stages in the transformation of thinking which the pupil of the spirit must achieve. From ordinary thinking, which initially forms the foundation for the study of spiritual science and corresponds to the first stage of modern initiation, the pupil advances through his meditative exercises to the second stage, 'creative, formative thinking'. Goethe possessed this capacity as a kind of natural endowment. Hence in the famous conversation with Schiller he was able to reply to the latter's critical arguments that he saw 'his ideas before him with his own eyes'.[2] This means that his thinking had already been raised from the intellectual to the visionary stage, without ceasing to be thinking. This is the most important quality of formative thinking.[3]

Rudolf Steiner also calls this thinking—in a Goethean sense—'morphological' thinking.[4] It was out of such thinking that he wrote, in particular, his *Philosophy of Freedom*, which is also why it was so little understood by his contemporaries. (See GA 79, 26 November 1921.) For this book cannot really be understood with ordinary, intellectual thinking.[5] And in another context he indicates that much of the content of the book *Occult Science—An Outline*, together with the whole principle of metamorphosis that came to expression in the capitals and architraves of the First Goetheanum, likewise had its source in this formative thinking (see GA 187, 1 January 1919) and, hence, as with *The Philosophy of Freedom*, can promote the development of this thinking within man.

The transition from ordinary to formative thinking occurs on the path of permeating and consciously directing the thinking process by means of the will. In the course of this a person must bring to realization what Rudolf Steiner, in the third chapter of the *Philosophy of Freedom*, calls an 'exceptional condition'. In this special state he tries to observe this himself with his now strengthened thinking. (One should not make the mistake of summoning forth what one has previously thought instead of thinking, for this would be like an ordinary memory process.) For what is involved here is a taking hold of the deeper power within thinking, which arranges individual thoughts in a logical order and transforms them into a single internally consistent organism of thoughts. In contrast to ordinary thinking, which in man is determined by sense-perceptions and is thereby bound to temporal circumstances, the second kind of thinking lives wholly in the living stream of time.[6] It is therefore independent of the body and can be defined as sense-free or pure thinking.

Through a further intensifying of the process the third step on this path can now be reached. This has to do with an *extended exceptional condition*. One must now, through an even stronger exertion of the will, suppress everything that one has experienced as a pictorial manifestation in formative thinking in order to arrive at an even deeper power, which lives behind the content of the second kind of thinking, is of a purely spiritual nature and extends beyond the limits not only of space but also of time. (See GA 79, 26 November 1921.) Only this highest power of thinking—and, with it, also the full consciousness of his ego—can be taken by the pupil beyond the threshold into the spiritual world.

Thus one can imagine that if Goethe had, out of his own power of formative thinking with which he also clairvoyantly beheld the archetypal plant, fully extinguished this imagination with the greatest exertion of his will in his consciousness, what would he have experienced? There would have been the various group souls of the plants, which he would have been able to perceive with his clairvoyant and clairaudient thoughts, the good as well as the evil. However, Goethe did not reach this point, because at this time the modern path of schooling which leads to this goal and is given today in anthroposophy could not as yet have been established. Hence he did not go beyond this first transformation of thinking. Nevertheless, one can with respect to Goethe but be amazed at how he was able to come through his own efforts—and without the help of anthroposophy. And so the Goetheanism which Rudolf Steiner developed out of Goethe's work is even today a firm foundation for anthroposophy and also the best training for the attaining of formative thinking.

One can also find an echo of these three stages of thinking in Rudolf Steiner's Foundation Stone Meditation. For example, references are made to the 'world of space', the 'rhythmic tides of time' and to 'the ground of the eternal'. The last of these is associated with the 'thoughts of worlds' and shows how man can consciously form connections beyond the limits of space and time with the eternal 'wielding' of the world thoughts of the spirit beyond the threshold with his thinking (GA 260, 25 December 1923).

This path of the transformation of thinking leads to what Rudolf Steiner calls man's 'growth of intellectual clairvoyance'. This new clairvoyance arises when one 'develops a heightened intellectuality not only for oneself but also raises it up into the astral world' (GA 130, 18 November 1911). When this happens, human individuals will in our time consciously perceive the etheric Christ in the spiritual world. (See ibid.)

Hence this path leads today to a conscious encounter with the etheric Christ, who in our time devotes Himself above all to that faculty in man which enables him to enter into a fully conscious relationship to Christ in the spiritual world. For this reason Rudolf Steiner is able to state: 'This is why, when people base their ideas on our spiritual science, there is so often an emphasis on the Christ impulse; for the Christ impulse has a direct relationship to formative thinking' (GA 187, 1 January 1919).

This can also be significantly confirmed from another angle. In the lecture 'The Etherization of the Blood. The Entry of the Etheric Christ into Earthly Evolution' Rudolf Steiner speaks of two streams of etherized blood that rise in every person from the heart to the head, the one from the individual himself and the other from the Christ Being. Rudolf Steiner specifically calls the first, human stream here the 'intellectual' stream (GA 130, 1 October 1911), because with it are connected the etheric forces that inherently make the thinking in man's head possible. Living thoughts from the spiritual world rise upwards with this stream and die in the human head, in order that man can inwardly take hold of and be conscious of his freedom in this deed of thinking. Rudolf Steiner goes on to explain that, when the two streams within a human individual are united in particular through the study of anthroposophical Christology, he comes to be able to behold Christ in the etheric body; for if it is embraced by the living power of Christ's blood, the dead thinking of the head can ascend to an imaginative faculty of perception and so behold the etheric Christ in the spiritual world bordering upon the Earth. Thus also from this aspect the path of development of human intellectuality leads through the study of anthroposophy and the transformation of thinking residing within it to a beholding of the etheric Christ.

This path is also the one on which the cosmic intelligence that in former times fell away from Michael can be brought back to him in a new spiritualized form; for through its connection with the stream of Christ in the course of its ascent the intellectual stream referred to does not come to a halt in the human head but continues to flow on into the spiritual world, so that the substance of the transformed human intelligence connected with it can be received by Michael in the spiritual world bordering on the Earth. That this process already begins at the stage of formative thinking (in that its bondage to space is overcome) is attested by the following description by Rudolf Steiner: 'The science which as anthroposophical spiritual science spiritualizes spatial thinking once more and lifts it again into the supersensible worlds works from below upwards, as it were stretches out its hands from below upwards so as to grasp the hands of Michael reaching down from above. It is then that the bridge between human beings and the Gods can be created.' (GA 219, 17 December 1922.) In these striking words the spiritualizing of spatial thinking cor-responds to the transition from ordinary to formative thinking, which—as we saw—lives in the pure element of time. And through the uplifting of the spiritualized substance of thinking towards the hands of Michael the transition is made to the third kind of thinking, whereby human intel-ligence finally flows back to Michael.

Thus one can say that in the twofold transformation of thinking that one can trace more fully and precisely in many places in Rudolf Steiner's work we have before us the *path* of inner development which leads most surely today to an experience of the etheric Christ. Human thinking is thereby also imbued with the power of Christ beyond the threshold; for only a thinking that bears this power within itself can perceive Christ in the form of His etheric manifestation.

★

The will pole is concerned above all with the development of moral qualities. The light of thinking is thereby sent down into the dark depths of the will. One could say that what is involved here is that the moral ideal grasped in thinking is now taken into the realm of the will in order to enable it to develop an inner impulse there.

Whereas the foundations for the one process already described can be found in the first part of the *Philosophy of Freedom,* where the focus is upon the nature of thinking and how freedom can be experienced by human beings, the outlines of the other aspect are described in its second part. Here the concern is with how a person can act freely in the world out of the moral intuitions that he has grasped in thinking. If one bears in mind here that Rudolf Steiner describes the source of love in man as the process of imbuing the will with thinking,[7] one can understand the esoteric and at the same time human-oriented foundations of what Rudolf Steiner refers to in the *Philosophy of Freedom* as deeds 'born out of love for the object' (GA 4, chapter 9), which are alone free.

Thus just as with the former process one encounters Michael with his outstretched hands as he raises the spiritualized human intelligence aloft in the spiritual world, so does one also meet Michael when one gazes in the other direction: 'And Michael has his own particular relationship to deeds springing from the impulse of love' (GA 219, 17 December 1922). For only such human deeds as have originated in moral intuition and have been performed out of pure love for the object are truly free and are, hence, associated with what Michael himself represents in the cosmos through his being. 'Michael wants to be the spiritual hero of freedom. He lets people act, but then receives what becomes of their deeds in order that he may carry it further in the cosmos, enabling what human beings are as yet unable to put into effect to work further in the cosmos.' (GA 233a, 13 January 1924.) Through this collaboration with Michael a person's free deeds, as described in the *Philosophy of Freedom,* become cosmic deeds which work on in Michael's realm for the future of mankind and the world.

This process of elevating human morality through the immersion of thinking into the realm of the will has a further consequence; for the human will is morally so strengthened by this that it is gradually able to break through the causality of the outer world from the spiritual side. In this way a start is made with the transformation of that power which governs the entire physical world as the law of iron necessity, of causes and their effects. 'We see the world we realize to be based on causal necessity as one that is perishable, and we recognize that the world that we build up out of pure moral ideals arises on the ground of that other world which is dying ... A morally pure will is the element in human nature that overcomes causality within man and therefore also for the whole world' (GA 78, 5 September 1921).

However, the causality referred to here has two aspects. In the one sense it permeates all natural processes and, hence, comes towards human beings from without. Here it would be equated with the death forces in nature; for only in the world of death (in the mineral realm) can it fully develop its unconditional, iron power. The second aspect, however, is spiritual causality, which manifests itself with no less necessity in human life and is called the all-embracing law of karma. But karma only has the power of iron necessity where it is determined out of the past, that is, fully immersed in the stream of spiritual causality and, hence, of an inner lack of freedom. This overall influence of karma can be broken only by a person's free deeds which have no karmic consequences from the past and are therefore not determined by it. It follows from this that a human individual can, through the moral transformation of his will out of intuitive thinking, also influence the causality of his karma in the sense of the higher good of the whole. By this means he enters ever more consciously into that realm where Christ is beginning to work in our time as the Lord of Karma.[8] Thus man gradually becomes His collaborator in the domain where karma is fashioned.

What will Christ's task be in His new cosmic office? Rudolf Steiner characterizes it thus: 'To ensure that our karmic account will be balanced in the future—that is, *made part of the cosmic order* with respect to that future time when we have found our way to Christ—in such a way that our karmic compensation will bring the greatest possible benefit for humanity, this will be the concern of Him who from our time onwards is becoming the Lord of Karma, it will be the concern of Christ' (GA 130, 2 December 1911).

The preparation for this karmic work with Christ has already been formulated in the *Philosophy of Freedom*, where the following observation is made: 'I do not work out mentally whether my action is good or bad; I carry it out because I *love* it. My action will be "good" if my intuition, steeped in love, finds its right place within the intuitively experienceable world continuum; it will be "bad" if this is not the case' (GA 4, chapter 9; italics Rudolf Steiner). In these two quotations there is a deep inner affinity between the 'cosmic order' of which man's deeds are to be made part by Christ as the Lord of Karma and the 'world continuum' to which the free human individual contributes his deeds of love in order that they can be truly 'good'.

Such a person who is acting out of freedom in the sense of the *Philosophy of Freedom* will already be working on Earth in harmony with the Lord of Karma. And if with the help of anthroposophy he has inwardly 'found the path to Christ', he will increasingly be a fully conscious collaborator with Christ in the domain of karma and also become able to meet Christ Himself in His new office.

At the end of the fourth part of the Foundation Stone Meditation there is a direct reference to this connection with Christ and also to the possibility that human beings have to do good deeds in the world out of their freedom.

O Light Divine,
O Sun of Christ,
Warm
Our hearts,
Enlighten Thou
Our heads,
That good may become
What from our hearts we would found
And from our heads direct
With single purpose

(GA 260, 25 December 1923)

For here we ourselves are acting and in complete freedom. But out of this freedom we now want to enlighten our hearts and heads with the light of the Sun of Christ, so that out of the collaboration with Christ as the Lord of Karma true goodness can arise in the world.

This work in the service of cosmic purposes consists in the following. In the language of the cited words from the *Philosophy of Freedom* the path to the Lord of Karma is associated with the development of a new faculty in the soul, one's own ('my') intuition which is wholly 'steeped in love' and, hence, aspires to the greatest 'world continuum' that is inherently attainable for a human being and which was brought into being by Christ and by His deed of the fullest freedom wrought out of pure sacrificial love in the Mystery of Golgotha.[9] If such a relationship to Christ and to His deed on Golgotha has arisen, a person can recognize the true source of his freedom, which he has now developed to its highest stage in intuitive thinking; and he knows that he owes *this* freedom solely to Christ and to His deed on Golgotha. Thus the path to the achieving of freedom, as propounded in the book *The Philosophy of Freedom*, leads to the present experience of Christ in the sense that Rudolf Steiner himself experienced

Him and subsequently brought to expression in the following words: 'That we can be free beings we owe to a divine deed of love. So as human individuals we may feel ourselves to be free beings, but we should never forget that we owe this freedom to a deed of divine love ... if we want to be free, we must make the offering of thanks to Christ for our freedom.' (GA 131, 14 October 1911.) It was this offering of thanks which Rudolf Steiner made in a way that no one else in the twentieth century has done.

If a person has not fully developed his freedom, he can still resist this spiritual source of his freedom, as Rudolf Steiner likewise indicates: 'And those people who consider that their dignity as human beings is restricted when they thank Christ for it should recognize that human opinions have no significance in the face of cosmic facts, and that one day they will be very glad to acknowledge that their freedom was won by Christ' (ibid.). But if, in the sense of the first part of the *Philosophy of Freedom*, a person truly recognizes Christ as the originator of freedom and accordingly— through cultivating the new, intellectual clairvoyance—comes to a perception of Christ in His etheric form, he can in the sense of the second part of the *Philosophy of Freedom* carry out good deeds in collaboration with Christ as the Lord of Karma.

Let us now return to our original theme. Although the development of thinking initially requires a strictly individual path (for one can arrive at an experience of freedom in one's own soul only as a separate human individual), karma nevertheless always works between individual people. Hence all real work in this domain necessarily leads to the social realm. For this reason a conscious collaboration with the Lord of Karma can only begin in a small human community, in order gradually to embrace ever larger swathes of humanity.[10]

Just as people will gradually be able to overcome causality in nature through such a self-transformation as has been described, so through their collaboration with the Lord of Karma can they achieve something similar in this realm. In this way karma is transformed from a law of iron necessity which brings about the just compensation in a person's individual destiny into a new influence of grace, in which everyone can collaborate out of his freedom. For what is true grace? Rudolf Steiner in one particular context gives it the following definition: 'What was defined as grace in the Christian sense was the soul's capacity to do the good out of its inner nature' (GA 103, 22 May 1908).[11] Accordingly the collaboration that has been described with the Lord of Karma, where the greatest possible good for the whole world is engendered from human freedom, becomes the new grace in the realm of karma. The overcoming of the law brought about by Christ on the hill of Golgotha[12] extends from our time onwards also to all karmically conditioned social relationships between people, in order with their free collaboration to create a new karmic order in harmony with Christ, so that it can become the expression of grace rather than of the law.[13]

It has already been mentioned earlier that the work on the overcoming of causality is enacted not only within man (karma) but also in the 'whole world', that is, right into outer nature. However, in nature forces of causality are active as actual death forces. Hence their overcoming is at the same time the beginning of the general overcoming of death. What is involved in this process is none other than man's participation in Christ's resurrection forces, which bestow eternal *life*. These can also be brought into the sphere of the social, where they likewise prove to be the stream of the life that overcomes death.

In the lecture on the etherization of the blood Rudolf Steiner speaks not only of the 'intellectual stream' already referred to, which rises from the heart to man's head, but also of the opposite stream which flows into man's head from his spiritual surroundings and can make its way down to his heart. Rudolf Steiner calls this stream—in contrast to the first—the 'moral-etheric stream'. It indicates the direction in which man receives moral intuitions from the spiritual world. It also corresponds to the path on which Michael would seek to enter human hearts in our time. 'Michael, who has been striving earthwards from the Sun on behalf of those on Earth who perceive the spiritual in the cosmos, seeks henceforth to establish his dwelling-place in the hearts and souls of earthly human beings' (GA 240, 21 August 1924). By descending in this way, Michael endeavours to extend his power through the forces of this macrocosmic stream from the head to the heart, where he seeks to appear within man as the inner Sun.[14]

Before we move on to man's third soul-force, that of feeling, the two processes already described need briefly to be compared with one another. As we have already seen, the first of these aspects has to do with leading the will over into thinking activity. The consequence of this is the reaching of the stage of pure thinking in the sense of the first part of the *Philosophy of Freedom*. Only in such thinking can true *freedom* become an inner human experience. The second process is concerned with immersing thinking into the realm of the will, thus enabling spiritual *love* as the foundation of action in the sense of the second part of the *Philosophy of Freedom* to be engendered within man. Both together, as freedom and love, form the future essence of humanity as the tenth hierarchy. For this reason the book *The Philosophy of Freedom* is the great teacher of mankind's future.[15]

These two processes can be described from another standpoint as the development of the new clairvoyance and the attainment of modern initiation. These elements were separated from one another in the old mysteries, but in the new mysteries they must be united with one another at a higher level.[16] They also encompass the two present paths to Christ, one of which leads to the perceiving of His etheric form and the other to the overcoming of the death-forces in modern initiation, which is possible only through a conscious connection with the Mystery of Golgotha and, as a consequence of it, with the Christ who is active in the spiritual aura of the Earth.

In the First Goetheanum (and also in the Second) these two processes are portrayed in the central motifs of the northern and southern rose-coloured windows. In the former we see the countenance of the etheric Christ appearing out of a budding and sprouting natural world to man in *Imagination*, an encounter to which man is guided by his guardian Angel. In the background one sees the barely perceptible form of a human double, who works primarily through man's dead intelligence but also possesses the strong will (see GA 178, 16 November 1917) to divert him from this high manifestation. On both sides of this central motif the aim of the epoch inaugurated by the etheric Christ is portrayed. So the opposing forces of Lucifer and Ahriman are not only brought into a state of equilibrium but gradually also led towards their redemption. However, this can only happen through human individuals who have taken the Christ impulse into themselves.[17] For his part, Christ goes before human beings in the fulfilment of this task, as depicted in the side windows. The power which has flowed into earthly evolution from the Mystery of Golgotha forms the unshakable foundation for this.

On the southern window we find the process of modern initiation portrayed. A human being sits there deeply immersed in meditation, preoccupied with overcoming the forces of death in his organism. This is indicated by the skull beside him, which is already outside his body. However, in order to overcome these forces he needs the connection with the Christ Being, that is, with the resurrection-forces that flowed into the evolution of mankind through the Mystery of Golgotha. Thus Christ appears before him in *Intuition*, who in His cosmic glory unites all the forces of the stars, the Sun and the Moon within his being. At both sides of this central image the mystery of the transformation of matter is depicted. What was formerly a bearer of death becomes transparent for the spirit after the overcoming of the causality that governs it through the forces of the Resurrection. Where previously skulls stood as a symbol of death, high spirit-beings now take their place. 'And the building becomes man'—this is the theme of this window. It points towards a future where man will become creatively involved in the universe even to the very transformation of matter through the power of the Logos dwelling within him. One can sense the following words of Christ as it were in the background of these images: 'Destroy this temple, and in three days I will raise it up' (John 2:19). What for Christ were these days between Good Friday and Easter Sunday signifies for humanity the whole of world evolution through the future aeons of Jupiter, Venus and Vulcan.[18] These are in truth the three cosmic days of mankind in order to reach the goal which it has been set as a new religion of the Gods by the Mystery of Golgotha.[19]

Just as the strengthening of thinking by the will entails above all a conscious *path* into the spiritual world, so the bringing of thinking into the realm of the will involves the engendering of new *life*. This arises within man because he has imbued his will in the manner described with the power of Christ beyond the threshold. Thus a Christ-imbued thinking and will form the foundation for man's new consciousness at the threshold of the spiritual world.

★

In the middle realm between thinking and willing lies feeling. This, too, must be 'en-Christened' at the threshold or, in other words, become a power that also leads today to Christ. Rudolf Steiner describes quite precisely how this happens in the lecture of 16 October 1918, which bears the significant title 'How do I find the Christ?' (GA 182).

Here Rudolf Steiner refers to how in our time incarnating souls have received a kind of reflection of the Mystery of Golgotha in the spiritual world centuries before their birth. 'People today, by virtue of being born into the physical world, all carry something with them that is like a reflection of the Mystery of Golgotha, a mirror-image of what they have experienced in the spiritual world centuries after the Mystery of Golgotha' (ibid.). As a consequence of this experience such souls bear within themselves a strong aspiration towards spiritual experience. However, at the same time they experience a profound sense of powerlessness with respect to truly reaching this goal of raising themselves up to the spiritual domain. This feeling of powerlessness is, however, a sure sign that such souls stand directly before an experience of the threshold to the spiritual world and are as though predestined eventually to cross it in full consciousness; for this feeling of powerlessness has its origin in the fact that the forces of death, which are associated only with the physical body, take an ever firmer hold of the soul in the course of man's further evolution.

When a person who bears within himself such an impulse from the Mystery of Golgotha deriving from the time before birth experiences this inwardly, he receives the strong inclination to defend himself against this death of the soul which threatens him and to turn now to the spirit with the full power of his soul. And if in this way a new connection with the spirit can be arrived at out of the deepest depths of inner powerlessness (in the course of which the reflection of the Mystery of Golgotha active in the soul is strongly influential), the person concerned will take the Christ impulse into his feeling and experience a kind of inner resurrection from the experience of powerlessness which has been described.

Rudolf Steiner describes it thus: 'But then if we can feel powerlessness and a recovery from powerlessness, we have the good fortune to have an utterly real relationship to Christ Jesus.' Through this occurs 'the redemption from powerlessness, the resurrection of the soul to the spirit' (ibid.); and someone who in this way 'can speak' from his own experience 'of the two events, of powerlessness and of the resurrection from powerlessness, is speaking of a true experience of Christ. Such a person finds himself *on a supersensible path* to the Mystery of Golgotha; he finds for himself the forces which awaken certain supersensible forces and which lead him to the Mystery of Golgotha.' (Ibid.) This can also be understood to mean that in this case the reflection of the Mystery of Golgotha that has been brought from the time before birth is raised up into waking consciousness and, hence, becomes a connecting thread leading to an involvement with the spiritual reality of the Resurrection. In this brief description the whole mystery of the threshold is contained where Christ Himself helps a person to withstand this trial and to enter the spiritual world with a feeling that has become clairvoyant.[20]

In the further course of the lecture Rudolf Steiner connects these insights with the experience of the nature of truth. In a short section he mentions the word *truth* seven times, thus achieving an extraordinary density in the presentation of this theme. This has to do with the 'great experience of powerlessness and the resurrection from powerlessness' with respect to the 'divine truth' (ibid.) which must be recognized by human beings and, hence, with the possibility of being inherently allowed to express the higher truths of spiritual research. In other words, the question is now how man can cultivate the *feeling for truth* as a new organ of perception for the Christ Being in his purified feeling, in order to win the victory over powerlessness.

With the attempt to approach Christ with his feeling as a new organ of perception, man experiences the decisive mystery with regard to the nature of truth. Through Christ's appearance at the Turning Point of

Time truth was transformed from a 'what' to a 'who'! For Christ is the first and only being on the Earth who could say of Himself: 'I am . . . the truth' (John 14:6).

However, one does not arrive at this higher, intrinsic relationship to truth through ordinary intellectual thinking, which always remains bound to the 'what' of the matter concerned. Only through the consistent development of what Rudolf Steiner calls heart thinking can one approach the living nature of truth. This thinking with the heart has a special quality. It can immediately grasp the true meaning of any particular situation without pondering it intellectually (and the organs of perception in the human organism do not need this either). 'For in order to determine whether something is true or false, whether one has this or that to say about a fact or phenomenon of the higher worlds, the kind of considerations that apply to ordinary thinking are not necessary; for it becomes immediately apparent. As soon as one is directly confronted by the fact or phenomenon, one also knows what one has to say about it and to others as well. This quality of directness is characteristic of heart thinking.' (GA 119, 29 March 1910.) And then Rudolf Steiner adds that everything that can be investigated in the spiritual world with confidence, that is, in accordance with the truth, has been found in this way: 'True impressions from the higher worlds emerge from such heart thinking, even though it often seems as if they were logical assertions . . . Thus even if we hear the profoundest truths of the heart in the form of thoughts, we must get used to the idea that these represent only the outward form behind which we see their real substance' (ibid.).

After the time of the great old civilizations which were guided from the spiritual world by the mysteries, with the appearance of philosophy in ancient Greece the truth of the 'what' became for the first time the object of human intellectual research. Socrates and his school were pre-eminent in seeking to establish truth on a rational, intellectual path and even engage in logical proof. Through this a decisive separation occurred between the sense-perceptible and spiritual worlds; for in the latter truth continued—as it had from earliest times—to revolve around 'who', always represented by actual spiritual beings who, as cosmic intelligences, are historically ordered and, hence, embody various stages of truth.

Through the appearance of Christ this archetypal principle of the spiritual world was directly manifested on the Earth. As formerly only amongst spiritual beings, truth now itself appeared among human beings as man. In order to grasp this decisive change not in an abstract, intellectual way but as an inner experience, human individuals must today develop within their souls a particularly strong feeling for truth, for this can enable them to experience truth as 'who'. If this is to be achieved it becomes necessary to find also in this domain the transition from powerlessness to resurrection; for people experience powerlessness with regard to truth for as long as they can only recognize it as 'what', thus causing them to be eternally aspiring towards what can never be wholly fulfilled. With the ascent from 'what' to 'who' with respect to truth, however, a resurrection from powerlessness is possible. This is at the same time the true experience on the threshold; for nowhere else does one experience inner powerlessness as one does in approaching the threshold. If a person is able to unite this experience of the threshold with the experience of Christ, he experiences the ensuing entry into the spiritual world as a true resurrection of his higher being out of the sheaths of the lower nature which formerly obscured it and rendered it powerless.

Only through the Being who uniquely has the right to pronounce the words 'I am the truth' can a human individual experience the source of absolute truth and, hence, the fulfilment of his aspiration for truth. In the terminology of the *Philosophy of Freedom* this means attaining to the source of all conceivable *moral intuitions*, which no longer have to be sought in the wide expanses of the spiritual world but were concentrated in one single human being, Christ Jesus, and since then can be found on the Earth by every human individual who through his feeling for truth has been able to gain access in his soul to the Christ Being.[21] In this way man's feeling can also be imbued by the Christ impulse beyond the threshold.

The fact that, in the lecture quoted, Rudolf Steiner brings this experience of truth into connection with the expressing of spiritual-scientific truths opens up to us a further perspective with regard to the quest for truth that has been described here; for a person who has developed this *feeling for truth* as a direct influence of his heart thinking will find that the entire content of spiritual science accordingly becomes a new language of truth in which people today can turn directly to the etheric Christ. Rudolf Steiner describes this quality of anthroposophy in parti-cularly striking words at the end of the lecture of 6 February 1917. The passage in question culminates in his call to all anthroposophists who were listening to him: 'So let us seek to acquire a relationship to spiritual science not merely as a teaching but as a language and then wait until we find the questions in this language that we may address to Christ. He will answer, yes, He *will* answer!' (GA 175, 6 February 1917; italics Rudolf Steiner.)[22]

It follows from these words that if a person approaches the study of anthroposophy not merely with the intellectual powers of his head but with the whole warmth of his feeling and, indeed, his heart, so that his heart gradually becomes an organ for the apprehending of truth, the substance of anthroposophy is transformed for him into a new language; it becomes a source of *inspirations* that lead him to a deepened connection with the Christ Being in the present. Through this he will increasingly be in a position to speak not *about* anthroposophy but *out of it*. Its substance has then become for him an unshakable truth, even if he cannot evaluate all of it from his own experience.

In some lectures from the year 1923, when he was already working on the preparation of the Christmas Conference, Rudolf Steiner spoke of the being of anthroposophy as a 'living being' of the spiritual world, to whom anthroposophists should have 'the greatest conceivable responsibility' (GA 258, 16 June 1923); and at the Christmas Conference itself he called this being by its spiritual name Anthroposophia, the emissary of the heavenly Sophia in our present time.[23] Hence the transition that has been described from 'what' to 'who' can likewise be cultivated through our relationship to her; for only if anthroposophy is transformed within us from a teaching to an actual spiritual being who 'knocks at the door of our heart . . . and says: let me in, for I am you yourself; I am your true human nature!'[24] only then have we understood it in truth *in a living way*. Once it has been inspired and permeated by Anthroposophia, spiritual science can become for us that language in which we can in our time—as described above—direct the most important questions of the present immediately to the etheric Christ.

★

We find all three ways of approaching the Christ Being that have been described in the artistic composition of the First Goetheanum. As already mentioned, in the northern rose-coloured window we find man's encounter with the etheric Christ; in the southern rose-coloured window there appears Christ's experience as the Lord of Karma at the height of modern initiation. The whole triptych is at the same time an artistic manifestation of the words 'In Christ death becomes life'. Then in the middle of the eastern part of the small cupola (if the First Goetheanum had been completed) the sculptural Group was to have stood; and—among much else that it brings to expression—what this work of art portrays is the process that has been described from the experience of powerlessness as a consequence of the incipient death of the soul to the recovery from powerlessness through the encounter with the Christ Being.

If one stands before this unique sculpture, one experiences it as consisting of two motifs. In the centre stands the Representative of Humanity with the adversarial forces, who cannot endure His presence, fleeing before Him. On the left is a side motif in which Lucifer from above and Ahriman from below reach out their hands to one another, thus causing the death of man's central heart region and, hence, the destruction of his soul.[25] This supplementary motif shows us the actual source of powerlessness, which we experience with respect to the spirit in consequence of the ongoing effects of the original sin that resides in our physical body. In the central motif, in contrast, we have precisely what Rudolf Steiner calls the 'resurrection from powerlessness' and a 'stroke of good fortune', which consists in that we are allowed to encounter Christ as the bestower of the soul's inner resurrection.[26] Thus in the artistic forms of the first building all three paths to Christ—through thinking, feeling and willing—are to be found.[27]

By way of a summary we can say: by imbuing our thinking with Christ we attain an imaginative perception of the etheric Christ; by imbuing our feeling with Christ anthroposophy becomes an inspirative conversation with the Christ Being; and by imbuing the will with Christ man can become His collaborator in the future social forms of human life through the intuitions of the Lord of Karma. Thus the modern path to Christ described here leads from the beholding of His etheric form to an inner conversation with Him and then to a conscious collaboration on the fulfilment of the aim that he has with regard to the further evolution of the Earth and humanity.

These three stages of approaching Christ are in our time also associated with the three faculties which a human individual acquires while still a little child—before the awakening of his individual ego—and in which the power of Christ exerts an influence mediated by the Archai while standing upright and learning to walk, by the Archangels while learning to speak and by the Angels while learning to think.[28] From this it follows that in beholding the etheric Christ the Angels are particularly active, as is confirmed by the fact that Christ Himself reveals Himself today out of their sphere; for the new clairvoyant consciousness that is necessary for experiencing the Second Coming has as its source the second, supersensible Mystery of Golgotha which took place 'in the sphere of the Angels'. (See GA 152, 2 May 1913.)[29] Similarly, a conversation with Christ is only possible through the mediation of the Archangels, because they so enliven the language of human beings—as already happens today in spiritual science—that a real conversation with Christ can take place in the spiritual world.[30] And if at the third stage we want to become Christ's collaborators as the Lord of Karma, we need the power of uprightness of the Archai and above all the help of the leading Arché of our time, Michael, who has given human beings a new karmic revelation through anthroposophy in order that they might be able to work consciously with Christ in the realm of karma.[31]

In the book *The Spiritual Guidance of Man and Humanity*, where Rudolf Steiner expressed himself in writing about the etheric Second Coming, he also spoke of how after the Mystery of Golgotha the three categories of the spirits of the Third Hierarchy—the Archai, Archangeloi and Angeloi—came under Christ's guidance in order to lead humanity on Earth further in this sense. (See GA 15, chapter III.) It is particularly these hierarchic beings who in the Foundation Stone Meditation are called 'Spirits of Soul', because only they can have a direct influence on man's inner being—which is why they also participate in the etheric Second Coming (the still higher hierarchies are too mighty for the human soul). They represent, respectively, the imaginative, inspirative and intuitive aspects of Christ's appearance and carry the impulses deriving from them to mankind. In his later life a person can through them also consciously experience the power of Christ which is active behind his thinking, speaking and upright walking, as precisely corresponds to the three aspects of the etheric Second Coming.

In the passage in the Acts of the Apostles where there is a description of Paul's encounter with Christ before the gate of Damascus, one can also clearly distinguish these three principal elements: the figure of Christ, His words and the aura of light around Him.[32] These same three elements are also to be found in the description of the etheric Second Coming by the seeress Theodora in the first scene of the mystery play *The Portal of Initiation* (in GA 14). This, too, has to do with a vision consisting of an image, the words and the ray of light[33] which derive from the power of Christ and work unconsciously in the small child as it learns to stand upright, to speak and to think. (See GA 15, chapter I.)

★

An altogether different aspect of the 'en-Christening' of thinking, feeling and will on the path of initiation is being addressed here, which consists in that one gradually becomes conscious of the three forces that work unconsciously in the small child and, hence, also of the threefold activity of Christ in our time.

In the sense of what has previously been said in this Appendix one can discern here three goals which must be achieved respectively in thinking, feeling and will on the path to the threshold of the spiritual world, if the crossing of it is to lead to an encounter with Christ. The *path* (way) of the transformation of thinking, as already laid down in the *Philosophy of Freedom*, leads us to the first goal. We approach the second goal with the development of the feeling for *truth*, which is achieved through the study of spiritual science, above all the summary of it that appears in the book *An Outline of Occult Science*.[34] The third goal is connected with the metamorphosis of the will forces. What is involved here is that through the work that people do on their common karma in harmony with Christ as the Lord of Karma a new, higher *life* can enter social life. The foundation for the attainment of this goal was laid by Rudolf Steiner at the Christmas Conference and in the ensuing karma lectures.[35]

Thus the three key words of the whole of what has been presented— *path* (way), *truth* and *life*—come together, words which at the same time represent three different accesses to the Christ Being and make it possible for the human ego to sustain and reunite thinking, feeling and will beyond the threshold out of the power of Christ. Furthermore, the way, the truth and the life—if they truly shine forth in man's soul in the manner described—are none other than the new thinking, feeling and will of man in which Christ now lives and works. And if thinking, feeling and will can really be imbued with Christ, the ego of man which is associated with them can itself rise to a higher stage of spiritual development.

In the words of Christ that sum up all these processes, the divine 'I am' is placed before the message of the way, the truth and the life: '*I am* the Way, the Truth and the Life' (John 14:6). This means that a person who makes the way a reality in his thinking, the truth in his feeling and the life that overcomes death in his will[36] is thereby ready to receive the divine 'I am' of Christ into his ego. Thus what matters today is that we consciously focus on what Rudolf Steiner refers to as the aim of the totality of his spiritual science for the present and future: 'If souls allow spiritual science to kindle an understanding of such mysteries and if our souls become familiar with such an understanding, they will develop the maturity to perceive in that holy chalice the mystery of Christ's Ego, the eternal ego which every human ego can become. This mystery *is* a reality; but people need to follow the call by spiritual science to understand this mystery as a fact, so that as they contemplate the Holy Grail they may receive Christ's Ego into their being. To this end they need to understand and accept these events as fact. But when people are increasingly well prepared to receive Christ's Ego [and one form of this preparation has been described here out of the essential nature of the anthroposophical path of schooling], it will imbue the souls of human beings to an ever greater degree. They will then evolve to the level where their great model, Christ Jesus, used to be. Only through this process will human beings learn to understand the extent to which Christ Jesus is the great model of humanity.' (GA 109/111, 11 April 1909; italics Rudolf Steiner.)

The very first orientation towards this goal is discernible already in the *Philosophy of Freedom*.[37] However, it arrives at its full development only in the book *An Outline of Occult Science*, which was written in the same year when Rudolf Steiner began to speak of the mystery that these copies of Christ's Ego are preserved in the Grail chalice and are today awaiting their distribution amongst individual human beings. It is in this sense that the words which in a certain respect represent the culmination of the whole book acquire their full significance: 'Anyone who learns to understand the deeper meaning of this symbol [of the Grail], as revealed through stories and legends, will discover that it most significantly brings to visible manifestation the essential nature of what was referred to above as initiation knowledge, centering in the mystery of Christ. Initiates of the modern age may therefore also be called "initiates of the Grail". The pathway into the spiritual worlds, the first stages of which have been described in this book, culminates in the "science of the Grail".' (GA 13.)

With these words the entire content of *An Outline of Occult Science*, which contains the outline of the whole of anthroposophy[38] and at the centre of which the description of the development of the human ego runs like a red thread, is oriented towards this modern mystery of the Grail. Whoever consistently follows this path of schooling of the 'science of the Grail' will come to the experience that Rudolf Steiner summarizes in the following way: 'Through this experience the pupil is initiated into the sublime mystery that is connected with the name of Christ. Christ shows Himself to him as the "great model of an earthly human being".' (GA 13.)

This perception of Christ as the great model of an earthly human being is precisely the stage that, in the words quoted above, corresponds to receiving a copy of Christ's Ego from the Grail chalice; for through this the pupil of the spirit will be able to recognize from his own experience 'to what extent Christ Jesus is the great model of humanity' (GA 109/111, 11 April 1909). In both cases the same reality stands behind the connection to Christ as the greatest model of humanity which reveals the connection of Christ's Ego to the human ego in the sense of the words 'Not I, but Christ in me'.[39]

Anyone who, in the manner described, has undergone preparation for this intimate ego-connection with Christ in his thinking, feeling and will and has thereby traversed the stages of the Way, the Truth and the Life has been chosen to come before the *Risen* Christ. This enables him to experience Him in the way that Rudolf Steiner describes: 'Those who are inspired and imbued by the Ego of Christ, the Christians of the future, will understand something else that *hitherto only those who have reached enlightenment have understood.* Not only will they understand the Christ who has passed through death, but they will also understand the triumphant Christ of the Apocalypse, resurrected in spiritual fire, whose coming has been foretold ... and who raises all people aloft with Him to the right hand of the Father.' (GA 109/111, 11 April 1909.)

Pre-eminent among 'those who have reached enlightenment', who have hitherto been enabled to receive a copy of Christ's Ego only at higher stages of initiation, was Christian Rosenkreutz in the sixteenth century (see ibid., 28 March 1909) and for our present Michael epoch Rudolf Steiner, through his initiation at the end of the nineteenth century.[40]

Thus from our time onwards this threefold path to Christ in the sense of the words 'I am the Way, the Truth and the Life' is, through the founding of anthroposophy as a science of the Grail, accessible to all people who seek the spirit. To make this possible, Rudolf Steiner wrote *An Outline of Occult Science* out of his Christ-imbued thinking and then, out of his Christ-imbued feeling, made its entire content visible in the architecture and artistic forms of the First Goetheanum as a modern Grail temple. Finally, out of his Christ-imbued will, he inaugurated a new form of community building among human beings during the Christmas Conference in the mystery of the laying of the Foundation Stone of the General Anthroposophical Society, in order to bring into their midst the essential nature of the Michaelic Grail that belongs to our time.[41]

As a modern Christian initiate Rudolf Steiner was able to achieve this relationship to Christ from ego to ego in addition to providing human individuals with an example of the influence of Christ arising from it in his own thinking, feeling and will as the Way, the Truth and the Life. Through this he made this threefold relationship to the Christ in our time as a modern path to Him accessible to any person of good will, with anthroposophy as a whole forming the cognitive foundation for this. If we take it into our ego as the Way, the Truth and the Life, Christ begins to be active within us. We will then be preparing our ego for when we may be able to receive a copy of His Ego.

This has become possible in our time because Christianity has itself reached the ego stage. 'Christian evolution has passed through a development in the outward physical body, an evolution in the etheric body and also one in the astral body and has developed as far as the ego. Now it must take into this ego the mysteries and secrets of Christianity itself. It must now be possible for the ego to become an organ that can receive Christ.' (Ibid., 15 February 1909.)

What is characteristic of this ego-stage of Christianity is that human beings will gradually become capable of receiving copies of Christ's Ego. If this is indeed to become possible there is a need for anthroposophy, which indicates the inner path to this goal. Thus anthroposophy is the foundation of the Christianity of the future.

Notes

Introduction

1. Rudolf Steiner's first reference to the supersensible appearance of Christ was in the esoteric lesson of 5 December 1907 (GA 266/1).
2. The window motif depicts a human being who is being led by his guardian Angel to an encounter with the etheric Christ, whose countenance rises up out of a budding and sprouting natural world. The dark double, slinking behind the form of the Angel, tries to prevent this blissful encounter. (See Rudolf Steiner, *Die Goetheanum-Fenster* (The Goetheanum Windows), vols. I and II, Dornach 1996). On the two side panels is depicted the motif of the redemption of the counter-forces through the pure love of Christ, as He exerts His influence after the Mystery of Golgotha in the spiritual sphere of the Earth. The beginning of this redemption is connected with two further supersensible revelations of Christ, which will in future times follow His appearance in the realm of the etheric. (See chapter 1.) Thus the second revelation will bring the forces for the redemption of Lucifer and the third the forces for the redemption of Ahriman. (See the rose-coloured triptych on the cover of this book.)
3. See note 1.

Chapter 1

1. See S.O. Prokofieff, *The Cycle of the Year as a Path of Initiation leading to an Experience of the Christ Being. An Esoteric Study of the Festivals*, part II, ch. 2, 'Of Michael's Participation in the supersensible Deeds of the Nathan Soul'.
2. Thus one can see that Christ comes to the Earth through the same three spheres (Higher Devachan, Lower Devachan and astral plane) to which He would again seek to lead the consciousness of human beings in ascending stages in the opposite direction in order, initially on the level of consciousness, to prepare for the future union of the Earth with the Sun.
3. It is of significance in this respect that the name Krishna is etymologically close to Christ.
4. See S.O. Prokofieff, *The Cycle of the Year as a Path of Knowledge leading to an Experience of the Christ Being. An Esoteric Study of the Festivals*, part XII, note 83.
5. In this Paris lecture Rudolf Steiner spoke for the last time about the content of the Fifth Gospel. This is also why this allusion to the 'Pauline method' of his research, together with the statements referring to the three preliminary stages, has so unique a significance.
6. According to F.W. Zeylmans von Emmichoven, the two central lines of the fourth part of the Foundation Stone Meditation—'Light Divine,/O Sun of Christ'—testify to this collaboration which exists *even today* (the first line relates to the sister soul of Adam and the second relates to the cosmic Christ). See *The Foundation Stone*, the chapter entitled 'The Pentagram and the Sun of Christ', English edition, RSP, 1963/1983.

7. In this connection it is important that Rudolf Steiner also speaks of his theory of cognition, as expounded in his writings *Truth and Knowledge* and *The Philosophy of Freedom*, as having a 'Pauline basis' (see GA 116, 8 May 1910). However, to enter into this particular connection would go beyond the limits of this present study, and it will therefore have to be discussed elsewhere.

8. Article entitled 'A Christmas Study: The Mystery of the Logos' (GA 26).

9. See S.O. Prokofieff, *The Cycle of the Year as a Path of Initiation leading to an Experience of the Christ Being. An Esoteric Study of the Festivals*, part XII, 'The Modern Mysteries of the Etheric Christ'.

10. See his *Chteniya o Bogochelovechestve* (1877–81). Published in English translation by Dennis Dobson under the title *Lectures on Godmanhood*, London 1948, and as *Lectures on Divine Humanity* by Lindisfarne Press, New York 1995.

11. Plato was still aware from the old mysteries with which he was connected that any philosophical or cognitive activity on the part of man must begin with the mood of astonishment or devotion. This condition belongs equally fully to the new mysteries and to the modern path of initiation. Hence at the beginning of his book *Knowledge of the Higher Worlds: How is it Achieved?* Rudolf Steiner devotes several pages solely to the description of this mood. For without its healthy cultivation in the soul of the spirit-pupil no real knowledge of the higher worlds is even remotely possible.

12. Although the word 'life' is invariably used here in English translations, the original Greek word is 'psyche' (= soul).—Translator.

13. In *The Philosophy of Freedom* there is a wonderful instance where Rudolf Steiner gives an indication precisely along these lines of the necessary connection of man's good deeds with the wider world. The exact words are as follows: 'I do not work out mentally whether my action is good or bad; I carry it out because I love it. My action will be "good" if my intuition, steeped in love, finds its right place within the intuitively experienceable world continuum; it will be "bad" if this is not the case.' (GA 4, 'The Idea of Freedom'; italics Rudolf Steiner.) See also S.O. Prokofieff, *Anthroposophy and 'The Philosophy of Freedom'. Anthroposophy and its Method of Cognition. The Christological and Cosmic-Human Dimension of 'The Philosophy of Freedom'*, ch. 6, 'Michael and *The Philosophy of Freedom*', Temple Lodge, 2009.

14. See St Paul's words about love in I Corinthians 13:13.

15. See note 6 of this chapter.

16. This also characterizes Christ's position within the Holy Trinity. As the divine Son He is Himself the essential embodiment of love. Out of His relationship with the Holy Spirit He beholds with wonder and devotion the indescribable mysteries of the Trinity. And, prompted by the world conscience, He wishes only to follow the inner voice of the divine Father: 'Nevertheless, not my will but thine be done!' (Luke, 22:42).

17. The War of All against All will take place around the year 7000. This can be calculated as follows. Each post-Atlantean cultural epoch lasts approximately 2100 years. The present cultural epoch will accordingly come to an end in the year 3500. The end of the sixth epoch will then be around the year 5600, and the seventh will be concluded with the war referred to around 7000.

18. Regarding the three egos of man, see further in chapter 3 of this book, and also in S.O. Prokofieff, *Das Rätsel des menschlichen Ich* (The Riddle of the Human Ego), Dornach 2010.

Chapter 2

1. Rudolf Steiner spoke about this, for example, in the lectures published in the volume entitled *The Reappearance of Christ in the Etheric* (GA 118).
2. Rudolf Steiner's last pronouncement about the etheric Christ, in connection with the year 1933, was in the lecture of 20 September 1924 (GA 346).
3. *The Spiritual Guidance of Man and Humanity* (GA 15).
4. In this connection Rudolf Steiner says that the path into supersensible worlds which is presented in this book 'is imbued with formative thinking' (GA 187, 1 January 1919), i.e. has its origin in and is based on formative thinking.
5. In the lecture of 26 November 1921 (GA 79) Rudolf Steiner says in this connection: 'In this *Philosophy of Freedom* that thinking is cultivated which one must systematically make one's own if one is seeking knowledge of higher worlds... This is a thinking which I should like to call morphological thinking, thinking in forms.'
6. Rudolf Steiner repeatedly emphasizes that the etheric Christ appears to human beings *on the astral plane*. (See, for example, GA 130, 4 November 1911.)
7. It is characteristic that in this context Rudolf Steiner emphasizes above all world evolution from an anthroposophical standpoint as something which can particularly contribute to the transforming of thinking. For in the picture of world evolution the Goethean notion of metamorphosis lives on in a higher and more all-encompassing way. If, in this connection, one bears in mind that the fullest exposition of this evolutionary theme appears in the book *Occult Science*, which Rudolf Steiner wrote in 1909, that is, in the year when he was himself able to perceive Christ's appearance in the etheric for the first time (see above), the inner relationship of this book—which according to Rudolf Steiner contains 'the epitome of anthroposophical spiritual science as a whole' (GA 13, p. 12, Eng. ed.)—with the etheric Second Coming becomes evident. See further in S.O. Prokofieff/P. Selg, *'Die Geheimwissenschaft im Umriss' und das Erste Goetheanum*, Arlesheim 2010.
8. The article 'The Activity of Michael and the Future of Mankind' (GA 26).
9. Regarding Rudolf Steiner's language, see H. Zimmerman's book *Vom Sprachverlust zur neuen Bilderwelt des Wortes*, Dornach 2000.
10. See Rudolf Steiner, *Das Wesen der Anthroposophie* (unpublished English translation in Typescript S 11 under the title 'The Essence of Anthroposophy', and S.O. Prokofieff, *The Heavenly Sophia and the Being Anthroposophia*, second English edition, Temple Lodge, 2006.
11. See also S.O. Prokofieff, *Die Anthroposophische Gesellschaft und das Wesen Anthroposophia*, ch. 1, 'Das Studium der Geisteswissenschaft als Begegnung mit dem lebendigen Wesen Anthroposophie', Dornach 1999.
12. In this connection it is also of significance that Rudolf Steiner gave the lecture-cycle in Holland the title *Supersensible Man as understood from the standpoint of*

Anthroposophy (GA 231), where in the context of man's life between two incarnations the entire perspective extended by anthroposophy over the spiritual worlds is portrayed with an unusual intensity.

13. GA 231, 18 November 1923. The concluding part of the lecture where these words appear was published for the first time in the note to the edition of 1982.

14. In this sense one can understand the observation that Rudolf Steiner added to § 2 of the statutes of the Christmas Conference: 'The Society is continuous with the Anthroposophical Society founded in 1912. With the same objects in view which were then defined, the intention is to create an independent point of departure, in keeping with the true spirit of the time.' (GA 260a, 13 January 1924.)

15. It becomes understandable from this why, in the brief sketch of his life and work that Rudolf Steiner—without any indication of place or date, but probably in 1913—composed, the word 'Intuition' appears again and again in characterization of the main thrust and principal source of anthroposophy. See Rudolf Steiner, *Hauptzeugnisse. Autobiographische Dokumente*, pp. 103–6, Dornach 2007.

16. See S.O. Prokofieff, *Rudolf Steiner and the Founding of the New Mysteries*, ch. 7, 'The Michael Age and the new Grail Event', second Eng. ed., Temple Lodge, 1994.

17. It is in this connection of significance that it was in 1909 that the theme of the copies of Christ's Ego, which from our time onwards more and more people will receive, was spoken of for the first time, that is, in the year when Rudolf Steiner wrote his most extensive exposition of anthroposophy, *Occult Science*, and at the same time had his own supersensible encounter with the etheric Christ.

18. See further in S.O. Prokofieff, *The Twelve Holy Nights and the Spiritual Hierarchies*, part II, ch. 3, 'The Building of the Inner Goetheanum as a Path towards an Experience of the Etheric Christ'.

19. See *Knowledge of the Higher Worlds*, the chapter entitled 'Some Effects of Initiation' (GA 10). The third lotus flower, in the region of the heart, is, it is true, not portrayed in the picture adorning the red window; but the fact that the power of Michael is already present and actively effective here in the heart confirms the development also of this supersensible organ of perception.

20. See further in chapter 5, where an explanation will also be given why the figure of Michael in the heart region of the human being portrayed in the red window is so small.

21. Another aspect of this legend, where it is described how the new Typhon reproduces the false offspring of Isis and has impressed his own countenance on each of the 14 copies, is in my view indicative of the danger that above all in our time threatens anthroposophy in the world, namely that of intellectualization, which would lead to its falling into the hands of Ahriman. Rudolf Steiner referred to this danger with reference to the end of the twentieth century in a conversation with Adelheid Petersen-von Sybell. The text of this conversation, entitled 'Rudolf Steiner on the Youth of the Future', is printed in S.O. Prokofieff, *Relating to Rudolf Steiner. The Mystery of the Laying of the Foundation Stone*, Appendix 2, Temple Lodge, 2008 (original German edition 2006).

22. It is also of significance that in this context Rudolf Steiner mentions Vidar, who will also appear with Christ as His servant; for it forms part of Vidar's present mission to lead the nature spirits into Christ's retinue. That the etheric Christ is being referred to here is apparent from Rudolf Steiner's hint that 'we reminded ourselves of this many years ago' (ibid.), this being a reference to the 1910 lecture cycle on the Folk Souls, likewise held in Kristiania, in the last lecture of which the relationship of Vidar with the etheric appearance of Christ was spoken about (GA 121, 17 June 1910).

Chapter 3

1. See further in S.O. Prokofieff, *Das Rätsel des menschlichen Ich*, Dornach 2010.
2. Rudolf Steiner spoke at some length about the relationship of the earthly ego to the higher ego in the lecture that he gave on 8 April 1911 in Bologna on the occasion of the Fourth International Philosophy Congress (GA 35).
3. See the previous note.
4. From this a direct connection emerges between Rudolf Steiner's early work and the path into the spiritual world which he described later in anthroposophy. One could say that the inner transformation of thinking which can be achieved by engaging with this early work is the best prerequisite for, and the surest preparatory stage of, the conscious and exact clairvoyance that can be developed on the anthroposophical path of schooling.
5. See the concluding chapter of *The Threshold of the Spiritual World*, 'Remarks on the Connection of what is described in this Book with the Accounts given in my Books *Theosophy* and *Occult Science*'.
6. On the basis that the second, astral revelation of Christ—like the etheric revelation—will last approximately 3000 years, we arrive at the end of this time (2000 + 3000 + 3000) at the year 8000, when according to Rudolf Steiner the union of the Earth with the Moon will take place. (See GA 204, 13 May 1921.)
7. This is not at variance with the fact that the seventh epoch that is envisaged here, which will be brought to a destructive end by the great 'War of All against All', will at the same time be one of the greatest egotism and of a corresponding moral degeneracy; for the higher spiritual impulses referred to here will be accessible at this time only to those human beings who through their inner development and moral qualities have been able to acquire a connection with the third supersensible revelation of Christ. They will form the spiritual elite of mankind, who amidst the storms of the War will already be preparing the next great period of the evolution of humanity (the sixth).
8. See GA 93, 11 November 1904, where Rudolf Steiner says that true Manichaeism will extend to the sixth great period of earthly evolution, in the preparation of which lies its fundamental task.
9. Rudolf Steiner speaks of how man's ego originates from the world beyond the starry sky in GA 201, 18 April 1920.
10. And in another lecture Rudolf Steiner expresses this thought in the following way: 'The pre-Christian saviours rescued mankind with divine forces. Christ

redeemed mankind with human forces [that is, with the powers of Jesus of Nazareth].' (GA 109/111, 11 April 1909.)

11. In the path through the 19 Class Lessons of the School of Spiritual Science, Rudolf Steiner has given an indication of how this happens.

12. See GA 152, 20 May 1913 and GA 194, 22 November 1919.

13. Rudolf Steiner speaks of how the entelechy of Jesus of Nazareth (the Nathan soul) had an 'Angel-like' nature in GA 149, 30 December 1913. See further in S.O. Prokofieff, *The Cycle of the Year as a Path of Initiation leading to an Experience of the Christ Being. An Esoteric Study of the Festivals*, part XII, ch. 2, 'The New Appearance of Christ in the Etheric, second English edition Temple Lodge, 1995.

14. See also chapter 5 in this book.

15. In the book *The Threshold of the Spiritual World* (GA 17) Rudolf Steiner brings the essential nature of man's true ego into connection with the 'super-spiritual world', which according to his description corresponds to Higher Devachan.

16. See also GA 226, 18 May 1923.

17. See GA 130, 1 October 1911, and also in chapter 2, where this process is described in detail.

18. See the Appendix, 'The Relationship to Christ Today', where this path of the transformation of thinking, which leads to the perception of the etheric Christ, is discussed in detail. The three present relationships to Christ that have been briefly sketched here are also characterized there at somewhat greater length.

19. Words from the Barr Manuscript, part III, GA 262; italics Rudolf Steiner.

Chapter 4

1. Hence in many contexts Rudolf Steiner emphasizes the affinity between memory-pictures and imaginations. See, for example, in his book *The Threshold of the Spiritual World*, ch. 2, 'Concerning Knowledge of the Spiritual World'.

2. Rudolf Steiner speaks about the tasks of Goethe and Schiller in the lecture of 29 July 1922 (GA 214). Thus in the course of his life Schiller was to make the transition from the abstract philosophizing which was habitual to him to the perceiving of true imaginations; whereas Goethe, who already stood firmly in the world of imaginations, was to come to a conscious experiencing of inspirations.

3. In order to explain this, Rudolf Steiner mentions in several lectures the story of a person who one day and for several weeks lost his memory and, hence, in this time was unable to control his life properly as an ego being. (See GA 234, 8 February 1924.)

4. GA 152, 7 March 1914. The Nathan soul (the being of the Luke Jesus) also directly participates in this process of the inner transformation of the powers of memory (through being imbued by Christ). See S.O. Prokofieff, *The Cycle of the Year as a Path of Initiation leading to an Experience of the Christ Being. An Esoteric Study of the Festivals*, part II, ch. 4, 'The Fourth Deed of the Nathan Soul and the Human Faculty of Memory', second ed., Temple Lodge, 1995.

5. In the lecture of 7 October 1911 (GA 131) Rudolf Steiner indicates that Christ's embracing of this karmic role amongst mankind will take place 'towards the end

of the twentieth century' and then continue until the end of Earth evolution. (See GA 130, 2 December 1911.)

6. Christ says Himself: 'Think not that I have come to destroy the law and the prophets; I have come not to abolish them but to fulfil them' (Matthew 5:17).
7. See also the Appendix to this book, 'The Relationship to Christ Today'.
8. An indication of the possible first steps towards such an 'en-Christening' of memory is given by the numerous biographical books that Peter Selg has published, which have the common feature that in each biographical study the influence of the Christ impulse has, either directly or through an encounter with Rudolf Steiner, a central place in the research.
9. See further regarding the spiritual union of mankind in the first chapter of this book.

Chapter 5

1. GA 159/160, 18 May 1915
2. The letter entitled 'Michael's Mission in the Cosmic Age of Human Freedom' (GA 26). Italics Rudolf Steiner.
3. Rudolf Steiner also speaks about this present mission of Michael in the letter 'The Michael-Christ Experience of Man' (GA 26). Michael has the task of bringing the primordial light of the divine revelation to human beings, without a luciferic element becoming involved with this revelation.
4. 'The Experiences of Michael in the Course of his Cosmic Mission' (GA 26).
5. See also S.O. Prokofieff, *The Cycle of the Year as a Path of Initiation leading to an Experience of the Christ Being. An Esoteric Study of the Festivals*, part I, ch. 3, 'From Michaelmas to Christmas. Michael and the Nathan Soul', Temple Lodge, 1995.
6. Rudolf Steiner subsequently described in his autobiography how in his youth he was himself fully consciously in the midst of this battle: 'So much the more conscious, moreover, was my inner struggle against the demonic powers who wanted to derive from knowledge of the natural world not spiritual perception but a mechanistic, materialistic way of thinking' (GA 28, ch. XXVI).
7. The fact that Rudolf Steiner speaks here not only of Christ but of Christ Jesus is likewise indicative of Michael's connection with the three cosmic preliminary stages of the Mystery of Golgotha, through which—as already described—Christ passed in connection with the sister soul of Adam (the future Jesus of Nazareth).
8. The letter entitled 'The Experiences of Michael in the Course of his Cosmic Mission' (GA 26).
9. The impulses which have their origin in the past are otherwise always luciferically tinged. Only through Michael's influence can the primordial light shine forth anew in the present free from Lucifer's power. (See the letter entitled 'Michael's Mission in the Cosmic Age of Human Freedom', GA 26.)
10. From this it also becomes understandable why the Foundation Stone of the Christmas Conference, which the members of the Anthroposophical Society were enabled to implant into their hearts after its creation, had to have a twofold, macro-microcosmic form; for its task is to unite both streams of etherized

blood—that of Christ and the human stream—in order to be the foundation for perceiving Christ in the etheric.

11. Rudolf Steiner says in this regard: 'Humanity will [from our time onwards] again grow into the land of Shamballa, from which the initiates derive strength and wisdom for their task' (GA 118, 6 March 1910); and in another lecture: 'All bodhisattvas draw strength and wisdom from the land of Shamballa' (ibid., 13 March 1910).

12. The letter entitled 'The Experiences of Michael in the Course of his Cosmic Mission' (GA 26). This 'deceptive, misleading splendour' of the ahrimanic 'intelligence of the present' can above all be discerned today in the modern world of electronically controlled artificial intelligence.

13. The letter entitled 'The Michael-Christ Experience of Man' (GA 26).

14. See further regarding the forming of this ether-sphere—which Rudolf Steiner also refers to as a 'spiritual ring' around the Earth (GA 112, 6 July 1909)—in S.O. Prokofieff, *The Cycle of the Year as a Path of Initiation leading to an Experience of the Christ Being. An Esoteric Study of the Festivals*, part IX, ch. 1, 'The Three Stages of Christ's Union with the Sphere of the Earth and their Reflection in the Festivals of Easter, Ascension and Whitsun'. The further relationship between the land of Shamballa and the sphere of the Earth becoming a Sun that is forming around the Earth arises from the way that Rudolf Steiner brings this 'spirit-sphere' into a relationship with the working of the Holy Spirit. (See GA 112, 6 July 1909.) The Holy Spirit, however, is also active amongst the bodhisattvas and among those initiates and Masters who are at a similar stage of their inner development and are therefore connected with the land of Shamballa. 'In the languages of the Near East it would have been said of a being such as a bodhisattva while incarnated on Earth that he was "filled with the Holy Spirit"' (GA 114, 20 September 1909).

15. See S.O. Prokofieff, *Und die Erde wird zur Sonne. Einige Zusammenhänge des Golgotha-Geschehens aus anthroposophischer Sicht*, ch. 6, 'Vom Schicksal des Bösen', Stuttgart 2011.

16. Compare with the letter 'The Michael-Christ Experience of Man' (GA 26).

17. After the Fall the Tree of Life became in man the Tree of Death (the system of the blue venous blood), which in future will be transformed into the new Tree of Life. (See GA 284/285, 21 May 1907.) This will happen through people consciously creating a new relationship with Christ in the land of Shamballa; for in this process the forces of the enlivened etheric body extend their influence within man to the physical body—first in the blue blood, which is thereby transformed from an expression of death to the expression of new life.

18. The letter 'At the Dawn of the Michael Age' (GA 26).

19. The letter 'The Condition of the Human Soul Before the Dawn of the Michael Age' (GA 26).

20. The letter entitled 'The Michael-Christ Experience of Man', italics Rudolf Steiner (GA 26).

21. In the language of esoteric Christianity 'from the East' also means from the direction of the spiritual world.

22. If one draws the axis of symmetry (from West to East) on the ground plan of the

First Goetheanum, one arrives at a form that is reminiscent of the four chambers of the heart.

23. Rudolf Steiner's sculptural Group consists of two motifs. In the central motif the Representative of Humanity is portrayed, while Lucifer and Ahriman flee from Him because they cannot endure His presence. In the left side-motif, however, the same adversaries are depicted—Lucifer working from above and Ahriman from below—who are 'shaking hands with one another', thus fully excluding man's middle realm. Thus in our epoch of the etheric Second Coming each person will have to decide which of the two paths he would wish to choose out of his freedom. The sculptural Group therefore also expresses the essence of this highly important decision that man has to take in the present. See the Appendix to this book, 'The Relationship to Christ Today'.

Chapter 6

1. See Rudolf Steiner's words quoted at the end of this chapter, p. 85.

2. If one adds to the year 2000 a further 3000 as the duration of the etheric Second Coming and an additional 3000 as the possible duration of the second super-sensible revelation, one comes to the end of the eighth millennium, which corresponds to the time of the Earth's union with the Moon. (See GA 204, 13 May 1921.)

3. These Western brotherhoods characterized by Rudolf Steiner should not so readily be equated with the world-wide organization of the Freemasonic lodges, although it is not impossible that these are used by, and made the instruments of, the secret brotherhoods in one or another context for their purposes. Moreover, Freemasonry in the modern world has such a complicated, diverse and contradictory structure that one can no longer speak of it as being a single entity. However, Rudolf Steiner emphasizes that for our time, when everything must be based on the free individuality, Freemasonry with its ceremonies inherited from olden times and no longer properly understood has outlived its time. A more detailed consideration of this theme is beyond the scope of the present work.

4. In the lecture of 18 November 1917 (GA 178) Rudolf Steiner says in this regard: 'The materialistic way of thinking is [today] in the process of increasing and will continue to increase for about four or five centuries', that is, until approximately the middle of the present fifth post-Atlantean cultural epoch.

5. It is unmistakably evident from Rudolf Steiner's spiritual-scientific research about these occult lodges of the West that, with their problematic goals, they work against the justified, positive tasks of the English-speaking peoples and should therefore in no way be identified with them.

6. This explains the secret aim of the great 'socialist experiment' in Russia in the twentieth century and subsequently in other countries undertaken by these Western brotherhoods, the prime purpose of which was that the right way of approaching the sixth cultural epoch was to be prevented. See further in S.O. Prokofieff, *The Spiritual Origins of Eastern Europe and the Future Mysteries of the Holy Grail*, part III, ch. 18, 'Regarding the Occult Streams of the Present which oppose

the Spiritual Evolution of Mankind', Temple Lodge, 1993, and S.O. Prokofieff, 'Bolshevism as an Initiation-Principle of Evil', *The Golden Blade*, 2001.

7. See S.O. Prokofieff, *Prophecy of the Russian Epic, 'How the Holy Mountains Released the Mighty Russian Heroes from their Rocky Caves'*, parts VI and VII, Temple Lodge, 1993.

8. The decisive difference between the two levels of evolution is that on Jupiter, Venus and Vulcan man possesses the higher members of his being (Spirit Self, Life Spirit and Spirit Man) as his own property. In the corresponding cultural epochs of the Earth aeon (the sixth and seventh) he merely experiences them as a revelation from above.

9. Still later, in the cycle on the Book of Revelation given to the priests of the Christian Community, he refers to 'ahrimanic demonic powers' and then says that 'one of the greatest of these demons is Sorat' (GA 346, 12 September 1924).

10. See, for example, also in GA 186, 12 December 1918.

11. Someone who, such as the author of these lines, has experienced the last decades of the Bolshevik regime in Russia can fully confirm the truth of Rudolf Steiner's words from his own experience.

12. This is how Rudolf Steiner refers to the Russian people in GA 185, 2 November 1918.

13. This arises from the fact that the sixth cultural epoch will have a clairvoyant nature, i.e. the new clairvoyance will be accessible to all people and will represent a decisive cultural factor. (See GA 186, 7 December 1918.) In the fifth epoch, by contrast, only specific, advanced individuals have this capacity.

14. Thus Rudolf Steiner says that the real culmination of Earth evolution will be reached by humanity already in the fifth cultural epoch. (For this culmination is connected with ego-development as the purpose of the Earth.) The sixth, in contrast—despite the general spread of higher spiritual faculties—will at the same time signify the beginning of the decline of earthly culture. (See GA 159/160, 15 June 1915.)

15. How seriously Rudolf Steiner took the situation that he foresaw happening in 1933 is evident from these further words from the same lecture: 'In 1933, my dear friends, there would be a possibility for the Earth and everything living on it to perish.'

16. In the lecture of 25 January 1910 (GA 118) Rudolf Steiner says in this connection: 'The first signs of these new soul faculties [which lead to the perceiving of Christ in the etheric] will begin to appear relatively soon now in isolated souls. They will manifest themselves more clearly in the middle of the 1930s, approximately in the time between 1930 and 1940. The years 1933, 1935 and 1937 will be especially significant.' And in the lecture of 6 March 1910 he speaks of how the first people with these new clairvoyant faculties will appear 'between 1930 and 1940 to 1945'. In the lecture of 23 January 1910 he directly specifies the year 1933: 'This is it which will appear around 1933, that He [Christ] will be seen as an etheric Being' (GA 125).

17. Quoted from Johannes Tautz, *Der Eingriff des Widersachers. Fragen zum okkulten Aspekt des Nationalsozialismus*, Freiburg 1977. See also Karl Heyer, *Aus meinem Leben*, Basel 1990.

18. See Antony C. Sutton, *Wall Street and the Rise of Hitler*.

19. One needs here only to think of the SS expeditions to the Himalayas organized by Himmler and the connections that were likewise sought with Tibet. (See J. Tautz, *Der Eingriff des Widersachers. Fragen zum okkulten Aspekt des National-sozialismus*, the chapter entitled 'Das Zeichen', Freiburg 1977.

20. See further on this matter in S.O. Prokofieff, *The East in the Light of the West*, part II, *The Teachings of Alice Bailey in the Light of Christian Esotericism*, Temple Lodge, 2009.

21. It is symptomatic in this respect that an organization called 'Ahnenerbe' (ancestral heritage) arose in Germany in 1933 which was integrated in the SS already in 1937. Its purpose was to study above all the roots of the 'Germanic nation', that is, its ancestral heritage. (The cruel 'anthropological' experiments in the concentration camps also subsequently formed part of this.) The expeditions of the SS to Asia and in particular to Tibet were likewise organized by this body. A distinctive cult of the dead was also practised in the Third Reich, which represented a kind of perverse ancestor worship. It is obvious that there is quite possibly evidence here of the occult antecedents indicated by Rudolf Steiner, that is, of a connection with or even direct inspirations from the Sorat demons that have been mentioned, which were sought in this way in the ranks of the SS and were associated with ancestor worship.

22. What is meant here is the heritage of the two centuries of Mongol sovereignty in Russia. (See S.O. Prokofieff, *The Spiritual Sources of Eastern Europe and the Future Mysteries of the Holy Grail*, ch. 16 ii, 'The Historical Symptoms of the Arising of the Muscovite State'. Hence Rudolf Steiner compares the Bolshevik tyranny in Russia with oriental tyrannies and says that it was even worse than the latter.

23. See the history and the text of the 'Mahatma letter' in S.O. Prokofieff, *The East in the Light of the West*, part I, 'The Teachings of Agni Yoga in the Light of Christian Esotericism', ch. 4, 'The Roerichs' Mission to Bolshevik Russia', Temple Lodge, 2009. Rudolf Steiner describes the deeper reasons why these Eastern 'mahatmas' accepted Leninism in Russia as follows: 'The fruits of Leninism do not represent anything so terrible to these initiates of the Orient, for these initiates of the Orient say to themselves: If these institutions of Leninism spread ever more widely over the Earth, that is the surest way to strike a terminal blow against earthly civilization. This will, however, be favourable to *those* people who through their incarnations to this point have created the possibility of living on without the Earth.' (GA 196, 9 January 1920; italics Rudolf Steiner.)

24. Of course, such etheric bodies no longer have a connection with their erstwhile possessors.

25. Atavistic clairvoyance includes—in addition to many other phenomena—also any kind of ancestor worship.

26. See further in S.O. Prokofieff, *The East in the Light of the West*, part III, 'The Birth of Christian Esotericism in the Twentieth Century and the Occult Powers that Oppose it', the chapter entitled 'True and False Occult Teachers', Temple Lodge, 2009.

27. In order to make this antichristian tendency in the Theosophical Society predominant—and this already happened in Blavatsky's lifetime, when she was

working on her second great work *The Secret Doctrine*—the distorted truth about the Moon's relationship to the Eighth Sphere, namely that the Moon is itself the Eighth Sphere, was initially publicized by her closest collaborator, Sinnett. However, the truth was the exact opposite: the good gods moved the Moon together with its solid matter into cosmic space so as to paralyse the Eighth Sphere and its influence upon earthly evolution. Through Sinnett's distortion of the truth under the influence of Eastern occultists, materialism became a considerably stronger influence in the esoteric realm. For if one places such falsehoods into the world arena, 'one will then be surpassing all earthly, indeed all conceivable materialism . . . Materialism is there imported into the occult realm; there, occultism becomes materialism' (GA 254, 18 October 1915).

28. In another context Rudolf Steiner speaks of the connection of the 'Tibetan, Indian and Egyptian initiation *of today*', whose representatives influenced Blavatsky in a one-sided way, with a 'store of wisdom' which today definitely 'belongs to a past age' (GA 158, 11 April 1912).

29. Annie Besant writes about this in her book *Esoteric Christianity or the Lesser Mysteries*, ch. IV, 'The Historical Christ', The Theosophical Publishing House, Adyar 2002.

30. See H.P. Blavatsky's article 'The Esoteric Character of the Gospels', published in the journal *Lucifer* in November 1887.

31. See further in Thomas Meyer, *The Bodhisattva Question*, Temple Lodge, 1993.

32. For this reason the author of these lines felt obliged to counter the further attempts of the left-oriented Eastern brotherhoods—through Alice Bailey in the West and Helena and Nicholas Roerich in the East—to proclaim the appearance of Christ alias the Maitreya Bodhisattva in the physical body with the truth in his three-part book *The East in the Light of the West* (Temple Lodge, 2009). Above all, in the Roerichs one can see how in certain cases the Eastern and Western brotherhoods of a left persuasion also collaborate. The Roerichs, who experienced a great upsurge of their fame in New York and associated there with many occult groups, then brought the letter from the Eastern mahatmas fully and unconditionally supporting the 'socialist experiment' which was initiated by the Western brotherhoods. At that time this quite possibly concerned the subsequent 'socializing' (in the Communist sense) of Mongolia, China and India, which could then be carried out only in Mongolia, in China and today also in Tibet.

33. In this context it is probably hardly necessary to mention that anthroposophists in particular are amongst the 'elect' with respect to the etheric Second Coming. For like no other people in the present they have through Rudolf Steiner been made aware of the most important event of our time and of the powers opposing it. Because of this, however, they bear the full responsibility for ensuring that people are not led astray by false messiahs but, rather, are prepared in the right way for encountering the etheric Christ.

34. This means that if human beings do not perceive the present, *first* supersensible revelation of Christ, they will also miss the other two which will together extend to the Earth's union with the Sun. (See chapter 1.) In such a case these revelations will be accessible only to initiates.

35. In the same context Rudolf Steiner mentions that, should this event pass

humanity by, beholding Christ in the etheric body and, hence, consciously working with Him within earthly evolution would remain restricted only to those few people who would have achieved the possibility of perceiving Him through a proper esoteric schooling.

36. The occult stream of Alice Bailey is without doubt the most significant further step since the failure of the attempt with Krishnamurti to have derived from the left-oriented Eastern occultists. See S.O. Prokofieff, *The East in the Light of the West*, part II, 'The Teachings of Alice Bailey in the Light of Christian Esotericism'.

37. Rudolf Steiner was surely speaking not merely humorously in giving the incarnated Ahriman a typical North American name, John William Smith. (See GA 195, 28 December 1919.)

38. See Vladimir Solovyov, *A Short Story of the Antichrist*, in *War, Progress and the End of History*, Lindisfarne Press, 1990. Also published separately by the Christian Community Press/Floris Books under the title *A Short Narrative of Antichrist*.

39. See further regarding this in S.O. Prokofieff, *The Encounter with Evil and its Overcoming through Spiritual Science*, part I, section 7, 'The Incarnation of Ahriman in the 21st Century and its Symptoms', Temple Lodge, 1999.

40. It is astonishing that already in the middle of the nineteenth century F.M. Dostoyevsky had a similar vision of the future which he presents at the end of his novel *Crime and Punishment* as the prophetic dream of the principal hero, Raskolnikov. (See the addition to this chapter.)

41. The etheric Second Coming will be at the mid-point of its influence at the beginning of the sixth cultural epoch. (The sixth cultural epoch will begin around the year 3500.)

Chapter 7

1. Rudolf Steiner spoke about it for the first time on 8 February 1913 in the Instruction Lessons of the cultic section of his early esoteric School (1904–14). (See GA 265.)

2. Here one can already discern the later inner experiencing of the Mystery of Golgotha in the biography and initiation of Rudolf Steiner, for only his perceptions of the Mystery of Golgotha were able to give him the key to the fulfilment of his life's task as characterized here.

3. In his autobiographical lecture of 4 February 1913 he reports: 'He [Rudolf Steiner] registered at the Technische Hochschule in Vienna and in the initial years attended lectures on chemistry, physics, zoology, botany, geology, mathematics, geometry and pure mechanics.' (*Briefe von Rudolf Steiner*, vol. I, Dornach 1955.)

4. In many early lectures Rudolf Steiner calls the path into the spiritual world described in this book the Christian-Rosicrucian path. (See, for example, the cycle *The Theosophy of the Rosicrucian*, the lecture of 6 June 1907, GA 99.)

5. From Edouard Schuré's introduction to his French translation of Rudolf Steiner's book *Christianity as Mystical Fact* (GA 8), published in: *Beiträge zur Rudolf Steiner Gesamtausgabe*, no. 42, Summer 1973.

6. Despite being presented in a wholly objective form, this lecture by Rudolf Steiner has a distinctly autobiographical character.

7. Lecture of 4 February 1913, published in *Briefe von Rudolf Steiner*, vol. I, Dornach 1955.

8. See Rudolf Steiner's words in this regard quoted later on in this chapter.

9. Both as a young man living in Vienna and also later in Weimar and Berlin, Rudolf Steiner was also intimately involved with contemporary art.

10. From his earliest youth Rudolf Steiner had abundant opportunity in Catholic Austro-Hungary to get to know the shadow side of the Church, which together with the whole civilization was steering in a materialistic direction. During his life in Vienna there were also various opportunities for this.

11. It is clear from these words of Rudolf Steiner that the word 'naturalistic' here actually means 'materialistic': 'Our materialistic age, especially since the fifteenth and sixteenth centuries, has not only made science materialistic but also the religious denominations of the West' (GA 52, 8 December 1904).

12. Rudolf Steiner later referred to the Michaelic background to the *Philosophy of Freedom* in the letter of 9 November 1924, 'Michael's Mission in the Cosmic Age of Human Freedom' (GA 26). And in another letter from the same volume he speaks about the path leading through *The Philosophy of Freedom* to Michael: '*When man seeks freedom* without inclining towards egoism, when freedom becomes for him pure love for the action which is to be performed, then it is possible for him to approach Michael' (the letter entitled 'The World Thoughts in the Working of Michael and in the Working of Ahriman', GA 26; italics Rudolf Steiner). In these words the quest for freedom refers to the first part of the *Philosophy of Freedom* and the deeds performed out of love to its second part. Thus working with this book leads a person *into the proximity of* Michael. However, in order consciously to meet him in the spiritual world, Rudolf Steiner had to follow the path through modern science described in this chapter. Regarding Rudolf Steiner's encounter with Michael see also in S.O. Prokofieff, *May Human Beings Hear It! The Mystery of the Christmas Conference*, ch. 1, 'Rudolf Steiner's Course of Life in the Light of the Christmas Conference', Temple Lodge, 2004.

13. The letter entitled 'Michael's Mission in the Cosmic Age of Human Freedom' (GA 26).

14. Regarding the precise time of this encounter see Peter Selg's investigation in his book *Rudolf Steiner und Felix Koguzki. Der Beitrag des Kräutersammlers zur Anthroposophie*, Arlesheim 2009.

15. This 'Manichaean principle' of the second, supersensible Mystery of Golgotha continued to be an active influence through the whole of Rudolf Steiner's life and reached its culmination in the year 1923 after the burning of the First Goetheanum. When after ten years of sacrificial work the Johannesbau (as the Goetheanum was originally called) was sacrificed to the flames through a criminal act of the opponents of the spirit, Rudolf Steiner transformed this act of the greatest evil inflicted upon his work and upon him personally into the radiant goodness of the Christmas Conference as the founding of the new Christian mysteries on the Earth. (See also S.O. Proko-

fieff, *The Occult Significance of Forgiveness*, ch. VIII, 'The Manichaean Impulse in the Life of Rudolf Steiner', third English edition, Temple Lodge, 1995/ 2004.)

16. Rudolf Steiner speaks about this on many occasions, e.g. in GA 152, 2 May 1913: 'The Mystery of Golgotha gave the Earth its meaning'.

17. What this signified spiritually for Rudolf Steiner, and what consequences it had for his further life, is described in S.O. Prokofieff, *May Human Beings Hear It! The Mystery of the Christmas Conference*, ch. 1, 'Rudolf Steiner's Course of Life in the Light of the Christmas Conference', Temple Lodge, 2004, and in S.O. Proko-fieff, *Rudolf Steiner and the Founding of the New Mysteries*, ch. 2, 'The Great Sun Period', and ch. 3, 'The Path of the Teacher of Humanity', second English edition, Temple Lodge, 1994.

18. Letter of 19 October 1924, 'The Experiences of Michael in the course of his Cosmic Mission' (GA 26).

19. Ibid.

20. If one considers that in 1879 Michael finally drove the spirits of darkness from the spiritual world to the Earth (GA 177), it becomes understandable that every person who aspires towards modern initiation has to traverse these ahrimanic worlds. Hence Rudolf Steiner says in his autobiography: 'Anyone who seeks spiritual knowledge must *experience* these worlds' (GA 28, ch. XXVI; italics Rudolf Steiner).

21. Letter dated January 1925, 'The Freedom of Man and the Age of Michael' (GA 26).

22. From the letter 'Michael's Mission in the Cosmic Age of Human Freedom' (GA 26).

23. 'This reawakening ['of the previously hidden Christ consciousness in the souls of human individuals'] is becoming the clairvoyant perception of humanity in the twentieth century' (GA 152, 2 May 1913).

24. Hence it is not fortuitous that Rudolf Steiner speaks both of the supersensible Mystery of Golgotha and of the receiving of the true ego at the abyss of existence in the same year (1913) and only then.

25. At this point one instinctively thinks of the dead members of the Western lodges discussed in the previous chapter.

26. See Johann Valentin Andeae, *Fama Fraternitatis*.

27. See the lecture 'In what sense are we Theosophists and in what sense are we Rosicrucians?' (GA 284/285, 16 October 1911). Here Rudolf Steiner explains that in anthroposophy the intention is not somehow to form a connection with the old Rosicrucianism still existing today as an outward tradition but to relate directly to its spirit and founder. 'We are Rosicrucians of the twentieth century!' (ibid.)—this is Rudolf Steiner's message in connection with his own mission. At that time Rudolf Steiner was still using the word 'theosophy' as a means of referring to anthroposophy. He also called the outline of his anthroposophy *The Theosophy of the Rosicrucian* (GA 99).

28. In the Book of Revelation the Lamb with the seven horns and seven eyes (5:6)— as depicted in the accompanying figure—corresponds to this sevenfold nature of Christ. (See GA 104a, 22 April 1907.)

And in another context Rudolf Steiner speaks of the six Sun Elohim who with Yahweh form the seven members of the Christ Essence. ('The six other Elohim, who, together with the seventh Elohim [Eloah], in their totality constitute the Christ impulse,' GA 186, 7 December 1918.)

29. See GA 130, 27 January 1912. According to Rudolf Steiner's spiritual research, the John who was the only disciple of Christ Jesus who stood beneath the Cross on the hill of Golgotha at the Turning Point of Time was an earlier incarnation of Christian Rosenkreutz. (See GA 265, p. 456, and also Hella Wiesberger's Appendix, 'Rudolf Steiner's research into the Hiram-John individuality'—ibid.)

30. Hence Rudolf Steiner speaks about the supersensible Mystery of Golgotha in a twofold way. On the one hand he approaches this theme from the perspective of earthly time: 'The Rose-Cross is a symbol for the second death of Christ *in the nineteenth century*, for the death of the [His] etheric body owing to the army of materialists. The result of this is that Christ can be seen in the twentieth century as I have often described to you, namely in the etheric body' (GA 265, 8 February 1913). But then he also characterizes the second Mystery of Golgotha in such a way that its lasting character comes more to the fore, so that a person can form a connection with it also today and far into the future. Thus Rudolf Steiner said in the autumn of 1918: 'Now, when Christ is to appear again in the etheric, when a kind of Mystery of Golgotha *is to be experienced anew*, evil will have a significance similar to that of birth and death for the fourth post-Atlantean epoch. In the fourth epoch Christ Jesus evolved His impulse for earthly humanity out of death; and one can say that what came to pervade mankind derived from the death which took place. Thus by a strange paradox the humanity of the fifth post-Atlantean period *is led to a renewed experience of the Mystery of Golgotha* through the forces of evil. Through the experience of evil it will be possible for the Christ to appear again, just as He appears in the fourth post-Atlantean epoch through death.' (GA 185, 25 October 1918.)

31. For this meditation Rudolf Steiner changes the feminine personal pronoun for the Sun [in German] into the masculine 'Er'.

32. See Margarete and Erich Kirchner-Bockholt, *Rudolf Steiner's Mission and Ita Wegman*, the chapter entitled 'Rudolf Steiner's Mission', English translation privately printed for members of the Anthroposophical Society, Rudolf Steiner Press, 1977.

33. In the meditation itself the path is characterized which, under the leadership of the Sun forces ('I hold the Sun within me'), guides the spirit-pupil through all

seven planets to the outermost sphere of Saturn. Then it reverses and descends from Saturn back to the Sun. In this way he experiences the latter as is otherwise possible only after death, no longer 'within himself' but he himself becomes the Sun ('I am the Sun'). The spirit-pupil who is approaching the spiritual altar is permitted this experience in order to experience there what has been described above.

34. See Friedrich Hiebel, *Time of Decision with Rudolf Steiner. Experience and Encounter*, the chapter entitled 'Laying of the Foundation Stone' (English edition, Anthroposophic Press, 1989).

35. Of course this is only *one* aspect of the significance of this sign. But the interpretation offered here is confirmed by Rudolf Steiner's indication to Ita Wegman that 'Christian Rosenkreutz with his hosts [pupils] came supersensibly into the "Schreinerei" during the laying of the Foundation Stone at Christmas 1923', which is also confirmed by the inclusion of the Rosicrucian dicta in the Foundation Stone Meditation. (See Margarete and Erich Kirchner-Bockholt, *Rudolf Steiner's Mission and Ita Wegman*, the chapter entitled 'Rudolf Steiner's Mission', Rudolf Steiner Press, 1977.

36. This group came into being through the initiative of these two people, which is why Rudolf Steiner gave it this name.

37. See the passage from the lecture of 11 April 1909 quoted on p. 25.

38. Quotations from the lectures of 10 May 1910 (GA 118); 30 January 1910 (GA 118); and 14 October 1913 (GA 152).

39. The chapter entitled 'The Pentagram and the Sun of Christ', English edition, Rudolf Steiner Press, 1983.

40. See the lecture of 27 September 1911 (GA 130).

41. Christian Rosenkreutz also followed a similar path in the long incarnation that is familiar to us (1378–1484): from the experience of Christ before Damascus to the historical founding of the Rosicrucian brotherhood in Europe and then, in the second half of that long earthly life (1459), to the new initiation which was made known to posterity by Johann Valentin Andreae.

42. GA 262, The Barr Manuscript, III; italics Rudolf Steiner.

43. See GA 94, 13 June 1906. In the following words Rudolf Steiner speaks of how knowledge of evil—and, on the basis of this, the 'fully conscious battle' with it—is amongst the most important tasks of the fifth post-Atlantean cultural epoch: 'What people in the fifth post-Atlantean period must become familiar with is the *fully conscious battle* against the evil manifesting itself in human evolution. So just as in the fourth post-Atlantean cultural period the battle was focused on the conflict between birth and death, so now is the conflict concerned with evil. Thus what matters now therefore is to grasp spiritual teaching [anthroposophy] with full consciousness.' (GA 178, 18 November 1917.)

44. 'An die Freunde', 4 October 1925. Published in English in *Anthroposophical Movement*, vol. II, no. 40, 4 October 1925.

45. M. and E. Kirchner-Bockholt, *Rudolf Steiner's Mission and Ita Wegman*, the chapter entitled 'The Michael School and Future Tasks'. (Translation of this meditation by Owen Barfield.)

Conclusion

1. See S.O. Prokofieff, *Die Anthroposophische Gesellschaft und das Wesen Anthro-posophia*, part II, 'Das Jahrhundertende und die Aufgaben der Anthro-posophischen Gesellschaft', Dornach 1999.
2. How strongly the three principal exponents of the two great conflicts in the Society, Marie Steiner, Ita Wegman and Albert Steffen, remained faithful to the Christmas Conference and, hence, to *this* task until the end of their lives is apparent from their own testimonies. See in this regard S.O. Prokofieff, *May Human Beings Hear It! The Mystery of the Christmas Conference*, Appendix III, 'Comments by the Members of the Original Executive Council on the Christmas Conference', Temple Lodge, 2004.
3. See Thomas Meyer, *Rudolf Steiner's Core Mission. The Birth and Development of Spiritual-Scientific Karma Research*, English edition, Temple Lodge, 2010.
4. And in another karma lecture Rudolf Steiner speaks more precisely about this time of 'waiting': 'And so the theosophical movement in Germany had to enter a more theoretical period than had generally prevailed in the Theosophical Society, and true esotericism had to wait. This was perhaps not a bad thing. For in the meantime fully *three times seven years elapsed.*' (GA 240, 24 August 1924–I.)
5. That Rudolf Steiner was referring here to anti-Michaelic demons follows from his remark in the same lecture about 'the enemies of Michael' who were active here (12 August 1924). These are connected—or are even identical—with the spirits of darkness who around the year 1879, that is, as Michael was becoming the ruling Time Spirit of our epoch, were cast down by him to the Earth, to the human realm. (See in GA 177, 14 October 1917.)
6. Regarding Sun and Moon karma, which are associated respectively with the forces of freedom (future) and necessity (past), see e.g. GA 240, 25 January 1924.
7. See S.O. Prokofieff, *Rudolf Steiner and the Founding of the New Mysteries*, ch. 6, 'The Foundation Stone Meditation', Temple Lodge, 1994.
8. See also the Appendix to this book, 'The Relationship to Christ Today'.
9. The letter 'At the Dawn of the Michael Age' (GA 26).
10. GA 26, Leading Thought 120.

Appendix

1. This is the substance of a lecture given for the first time on 16 March 2007 in Colmar and thereafter in various other places under the title 'Experiences of Christ's Activity Today'. In response to many requests from listeners and because of the thematic relationship to the content of this book, the lecture appears here in written form.
2. Quoted from GA 28, chapter V.
3. In his further characterization of formative thinking, Rudolf Steiner also speaks of how it is strengthened through the corresponding spiritual-scientific exercises to the point of perceiving the etheric panorama of the whole of a past earthly life extending back potentially to birth.
4. See further in chapter 2.

5. A classic example of this was Eduard von Hartmann. See his marginal comment on the *Philosophy of Freedom* published in GA 4a.

6. From this it becomes clear that Goethe, without being precisely aware of the fact, was in a special exceptional condition through his unique soul disposition, thus enabling him to perceive the archetypal plant.

7. See in GA 202, 19 December 1920. In this connection one must clearly distinguish purely spiritual love as man's highest creative power from what one associates with feeling in general. This can also be related to world evolution as a whole. Thus what man bears within himself today as the will has its spiritual origin on Old Saturn. Similarly, human feeling derives from Old Sun, thinking from Old Moon and true love arises as the gift of the Spirits of Form only on the Earth. (See GA 121, 11 June 1910.)

8. In the lecture of 7 October 1911 (GA 131) Rudolf Steiner indicates that Christ's real activity as the Lord of Karma will begin at the end of the twentieth century. His actual words were these: 'Thus in the course of the twentieth century, towards its end, a significant event will take place ... namely, that Christ becomes the Lord of Karma for the evolution of mankind.' This does not rule out the fact that the spiritual preparation for this new task of Christ has already begun with His appearance in the etheric body (from the 1930s onwards).

9. The 'world continuum' in which the Mystery of Golgotha stands encompasses the whole evolution from Old Saturn to Vulcan and even extends beyond it. See S.O. Prokofieff, *The Mystery of the Resurrection in the Light of Anthroposophy*, chapter II, 'Easter, Ascension and Whitsun in the Light of Anthroposophy', Temple Lodge, 2010.

10. Herein lies the essential esoteric reason for, and at the same time the task of, the General Anthroposophical Society founded at the Christmas Conference of 1923/24, to which the substance of the karma lectures was therefore entrusted by Rudolf Steiner.

11. See also GA 342, 15 June 1921.

12. Rudolf Steiner says in this regard: 'In ancient times there was the law. The law became grace through Christ, in that it is lifted out from man's own breast.' (GA 97, 30 March 1906.) Also in another context Rudolf Steiner speaks of how 'Christ is the God who [after the Mystery of Golgotha] can also hold sway within man and makes it possible for man to become his own law-giver through grace' (GA 54, 22 February 1906). In the *Philosophy of Freedom* Rudolf Steiner had already pointed in the same direction, for example when he writes: 'I feel no compulsion of moral precepts, but I want simply to carry out what lies within me' (GA 4, ch.9), or 'what my moral love itself will recognize as law' (ibid.). Elsewhere Rudolf Steiner indicates that on this path even karma itself is overcome. Thus he speaks of a true Master: 'He stands above karma' (GA 93a, 24 October 1905), even though these words should be taken only as the suggestion of a development and not in an absolute sense. One could also say: the Master overcomes the forces of causality in his destiny. For this, however, he needs the relationship to Christ that has been described.

13. When Rudolf Steiner writes in the *Philosophy of Freedom* that man is only free if he performs his deeds out of love ('only when I follow my love for my objective

is it I myself who act ... I acknowledge no external principle for my action, because I have found in myself the ground for my action, namely my love of the action', ch. 9), this is already a clear hint of what is involved here.

14. In another context Rudolf Steiner writes in this connection: 'Michael, who has spoken "from above", can be heard "from within [man]", where he will make his new abode' (from the letter 'The Condition of the Human Soul before the Dawn of the Michael Age', GA 26). Because Michael is therefore being spoken of as being an 'inner Sun' within man, it follows that he will take up his new abode in human hearts; for the inner Sun can shine only within man's heart.

15. It is in this sense that Rudolf Steiner's answer to Walter Johannes Stein's question should be understood: 'What will remain of your work after several thousand years?'—'Only the *Philosophy of Freedom*.' (From the 'Hague Conversation', published in *W.J. Stein/Rudolf Steiner, Dokumentation eines wegweisenden Zusammenwirkens*, Dornach 1985.)

16. Rudolf Steiner writes in this connection: 'In modern times the powers guiding humanity have to deal with the special task of bringing about a balance between the two principles of clairvoyance and initiation' (GA 15, chapter II).

17. It is already possible for many people in our time to collaborate in the redemption of Lucifer. (See GA 110, 18 April 1909–II.) The future redemption of Ahriman, on the other hand, is possible only for initiates. Rudolf Steiner gives an indication of this in Benedictus's concluding monologue at the end of the fourth mystery play *The Soul's Awakening* (GA 14).

18. See regarding this in S.O. Prokofieff, *The Mystery of the Resurrection in the Light of Anthroposophy*, ch. II, 'Easter, Ascension and Whitsun in the Light of Anthroposophy', Temple Lodge, 2010.

19. Rudolf Steiner speaks about the goal of human evolution as a religion of the Gods (hierarchies) in the spiritual world in the lecture of 10 April 1914 (GA 153).

20. Rudolf Steiner describes at some length how feeling can be transformed into a spiritual organ of perception which receives true inspirations in the book *The Stages of Higher Knowledge*, the chapter entitled 'Inspiration' (GA 12).

21. Rudolf Steiner refers in the following words to the mystery of the transition from the source of moral intuitions from the cosmos (from the Sun) to the Earth through Christ's appearance on it: 'They [the old initiates] conceived of the Sun as a Spirit Being. Those who were initiated regarded this Spirit Being [Christ before His descent to the Earth] as the source of all morality. So when I spoke in my *Philosophy of Freedom* of moral intuitions *being drawn from this source*, they are drawn from within the Earth [because their cosmic source—the Christ—has united Himself with human beings through the Mystery of Golgotha]; they begin to shine forth from human beings, from what can live in human individuals by way of moral enthusiasm' (GA 202, 18 December 1920).

22. A longer quotation from this part of the lecture can be found in chapter 2.

23. See S.O. Prokofieff, *The Heavenly Sophia and the Being Anthroposophia*, Temple Lodge, 1996/2006.

24. GA 231, 18 November 1923.

25. It is of significance in this respect that in the paintings of the small cupola— directly above the place occupied by the sculptural Group—only the central

motif (Christ between Lucifer and Ahriman) is depicted, without the side motif. For what on the Earth still requires man's free decision (to decide between what is indicated by the two motifs) Christ Himself has already resolved for the world through His deed on Golgotha (three crosses in the painting).

26. In several lectures Rudolf Steiner refers to the missed opportunity to form a connection with Christ on the Earth as a great misfortune in human destiny. (See, for example, GA 182, 16 October 1918.)

27. On the path of schooling, one can on approaching the threshold experience powerlessness and the recovery from it in all three realms: as powerlessness in thinking, acquiring knowledge of the spiritual world; as powerlessness in feeling, finding divine truth; and as powerlessness in the will sphere, being able to do the good in life. In the manner described here all three forms of powerlessness can be overcome within one's soul out of the power of Christ.

28. See chapter 3.

29. In the northern rose-coloured glass window of the Goetheanum where the encounter with the etheric Christ is depicted, man is led to this experience by an Angel. (See regarding this in the present Appendix.)

30. Regarding the relationship of the Archangels to human language, which can today be enlivened by Christ, see GA 224, 13 April 1923.

31. Later on in this Appendix the fourth stage of this path to Christ—associated with man's ego—is characterized. It also has a relationship to the hierarchic ordering of the cosmos. What is meant here is a particular category of Archai or Spirits of Personality, who bestowed the substance of the ego on man at the beginning of earthly evolution and are today in the course of becoming the 'new creators', that is, ascending to the stage of the Spirits of Form (Elohim) (see GA 187, 31 December 1918). For only with the help of these sublime spirits amongst whom Christ Himself once dwelt on the Sun will the wholly new connection that is arising between the human ego and Christ's Ego from our time onwards be possible. (See below.)

32. See Acts 9:3–7. These verses respectively have to do with the light (verse 3), the voice (verse 4) and only at the end with the figure of Christ (verses 5–6).

33. Hence in his lectures Rudolf Steiner again and again compares the etheric Second Coming with the vision of Christ that Paul had before Damascus. (See, for example, GA 125, 23 January 1910.)

34. Regarding the uniqueness of the description of the main content of anthroposophy in *An Outline of Occult Science*, see S.O. Prokofieff, 'Die Geheimwissenschaft im Umriss und das Mysterium von Golgotha', published in the anthology S.O. Prokofieff/P. Selg, *Die Christologie des Buches 'Die Geheimwissenschaft im Umriss'*, Arlesheim 2010.

35. This 'en-Christening' of thinking, feeling and willing is to be found in the three microcosmic sections of the first three parts of the Foundation Stone Meditation. Thus in the respective three parts we find the words 'truly think/from the ground of the spirit in man', 'truly feel/'mid the weaving of the soul of man' and 'truly live/in the all-world-being of man' (GA 260, 25 December 1923). These three soul-forces are held together after the crossing of the threshold by the 'Sun of Christ' of the fourth part.

36. The first part of the Foundation Stone Meditation concludes with the word 'live' instead of the word 'will' because in the spiritual world the will becomes for us an element of life.

37. That the entire content of *The Philosophy of Freedom* is oriented towards modern man's attaining of the higher ego is discussed at greater length in S.O. Prokofieff, *Anthroposophy and 'The Philosophy of Freedom'. Anthroposophy and its Method of Cognition. The Christological and Cosmic-Human Dimensions of 'The Philosophy of Freedom'*, ch. 14, '*The Philosophy of Freedom* and the modern Knowledge of the Grail', Temple Lodge, 2009. The ascent to this stage is, however, necessary in order to become a bearer of a copy of Christ's Ego in the sense of the modern Grail mysteries.

38. In the last foreword to the book, which Rudolf Steiner wrote only a few weeks before his death, this fact is formulated as follows: 'The book is after all an epitome of anthroposophy as a whole' (GA 13).

39. Galatians 2:20, following Rudolf Steiner's free translation.

40. See further in S.O. Prokofieff, *May Human Beings Hear It! The Mystery of the Christmas Conference*, ch. 1, 'Rudolf Steiner's Course of Life in the Light of the Christmas Conference', Temple Lodge, 2004.

41. See S.O. Prokofieff, *Rudolf Steiner and the Founding of the New Mysteries*, ch. 7, 'The Michael Epoch and the New Grail Event', Temple Lodge, 1994.

Bibliography

The following list of Rudolf Steiner's works includes the books and lectures referred to in the present book, and is arranged in accordance with the complete edition of his works. Where a German title is given, this means that the volume concerned has not been translated in its entirety or that the lectures are included in more than one published book. Where this is the case, indications are given as to where individual lectures that have been translated may be found. Translations from Rudolf Steiner's books and lectures in the present volume have, with a few exceptions, been made or edited by the translator.

GA 4	*The Philosophy of Freedom* or *Intuitive Thinking on a Spiritual Path*
GA 10	*Knowledge of the Higher Worlds* or *How to Know Higher Worlds*
GA 12	*The Stages of Higher Knowledge*
GA 13	*Occult Science* or *An Outline of Esoteric Science*
GA 14	*The Four Mystery Plays*
GA 15	*The Spiritual Guidance of Man and Humanity*
GA 26	*Anthroposophical Leading Thoughts*
GA 28	*The Course of My Life* or *Autobiography*
GA 35	*Philosophie und Anthroposophie*
	The lecture of 8 April 1911 is published in *Esoteric Development.*
GA 52	*The History of Hypnotism and Somnambulism* or *History of Spiritism*
GA 54	*Die Welträtsel und die Anthroposophie*
GA 78	*Fruits of Anthroposophy*
GA 79	*Paths to Knowledge of Higher Worlds*
GA 84	*Was wollte das Goetheanum und was soll die Anthroposophie?*
	The lecture of 9 April 1923 is available in Typescript S 34.
GA 93	*The Temple Legend*
GA 93a	*Foundations of Esotericism*
GA 94	*An Esoteric Cosmology*
GA 96	*Original Impulses for the Science of the Spirit*
GA 99	*Theosophy of the Rosicrucian* or *Rosicrucian Wisdom*
GA 103	*The Gospel of St John*
GA 104a	*Reading the Pictures of the Apocalypse*
GA 109/111	*The Principle of Spiritual Economy* or *Rosicrucian Esotericism*
GA 112	*The Gospel of St John in its Relation to the Other Gospels*
GA 114	*The Gospel of St Luke*
GA 116	*The Christ Impulse and the Development of Ego Consciousness*
GA 118	*The Reappearance of Christ in the Etheric*
GA 119	*Macrocosm and Microcosm*
GA 121	*The Mission of Folk Souls*
GA 123	*The Gospel of St Matthew*
GA 125	*Wege und Ziele des geistigen Menschen*

	An extract from the lecture of 23 January 1910 is available in Typescript EN 46.
GA 130	*Esoteric Christianity*
GA 131	*From Jesus to Christ*
GA 133	*Earthly and Cosmic Man*
GA 137	*Man in the Light of Occultism, Theosophy and Philosophy*
GA 142	*The Bhagavad Gita and the Epistles of St Paul*
GA 147	*Secrets of the Threshold*
GA 148	*The Fifth Gospel*
GA 149	*Christ and the Spiritual World and the Search for the Holy Grail*
GA 152	*Approaching the Mystery of Golgotha*
GA 153	*The Inner Nature of Man and the Life between Death and a New Birth*
GA 155	*Christ and the Human Soul* or *The Spiritual Foundation of Morality*
GA 156	*Occult Reading and Occult Hearing*
GA 158	*Der Zusammenhang des Menschen mit der elementarischen Welt*
	The lecture of 9 November 1914 is available in Typescript Z 144.
GA 159/160	*Das Geheimnis des Todes*
	The lecture of 15 June 1915 is published under the title *Preparing for the Sixth Epoch*, and that of 18 May 1915 is included in *Christ in Relation to Lucifer and Ahriman*.
GA 165	*Die geistige Vereinigung der Menschheit durch den Christus-Impuls*
	The lecture of 19 December 1915 is included in *Festivals of the Seasons* and published under the title *The Christmas Thought and the Mystery of the Ego*.
GA 174	*The Karma of Untruthfulness, vol. II*
GA 174a	*Mitteleuropa zwischen Ost und West*
	The lecture of 17 February 1918 is included in *The Mission of the Archangel Michael*.
GA 175	*Bausteine zu einer Erkenntnis des Mysteriums von Golgotha*
	The lecture of 6 February 1917 is included in *Cosmic and Human Metamorphoses*.
GA 177	*The Fall of the Spirits of Darkness*
GA 178	*Secret Brotherhoods*
GA 180	*Ancient Myths—Their Meaning and Connection with Evolution*
GA 182	*Der Tod als Lebenswandlung*
	The lecture of 16 October 1918 is published under the title *How do I find the Christ?*
GA 184	*Die Polarität von Dauer und Entwickelung im Menschenleben*
	The lecture of 11 October 1918 is included in *Three Streams in the Evolution of Mankind*.
GA 185	*From Symptom to Reality in Modern History*
GA 186	*The Challenge of the Times*
GA 187	*How Can Mankind Find the Christ Again?*
GA 191	*Soziales Verständnis aus geisteswissenschaftlicher Erkenntnis*
	The lecture of 15 November 1919 is included in *Influences of Lucifer and Ahriman*

GA 192   *Geisteswissenschaftliche Behandlung sozialer und pädagogischer Fragen*
GA 194   *The Mission of the Archangel Michael*
GA 195   *Cosmic New Year*
           The lecture of 28 December 1919 is also published under the title
           Incarnation of Ahriman.
GA 197   *Polarities in the Evolution of Mankind*
GA 202   *Die Brücke zwischen der Weltgeistigkeit und dem Physischen des Menschen*
           The lectures of 17, 18 and 19 December 1920 are published under the
           title *The Bridge between Universal Spirituality and the Physical Constitution*
           The lecture of 24 December 1920 can be found in *The Search for the
           New Isis.*
GA 204   *Materialism and the Task of Anthroposophy*
GA 211   *Das Sonnenmysterium und das Mysterium von Tod und Auferstehung*
GA 214   *The Mystery of the Trinity*
GA 218   *Geistige Zusammenhänge in der Gestaltung des menschlichen Organismus*
           The lecture of 19 November 1922 is included in *Man's Life on Earth
           and in the Spiritual World.*
GA 219   *Man and the World of Stars*
GA 223   The lectures cited in this book are included in *Michaelmas and the Soul
           Forces of Man.*
GA 224   *Die menschliche Seele in ihrem Zusammenhang mit göttlichen Individualitäten*
           The lecture of 13 April 1923 was published in *The Golden Blade* in
           1973.
GA 226   *Man's Being, his Destiny and World Evolution*
GA 227   *The Evolution of the World and of Humanity* or *Evolution of Consciousness*
GA 231   *Supersensible Man*
GA 233a   The lectures cited in this book are included in *Rosicrucianism and
           Modern Initiation*
GA 237   *Karmic Relationships vol. III*
GA 240   *Karmic Relationships vols VI and VIII*
GA 254   *The Occult Movement in the Nineteenth Century*
GA 258   *The Anthroposophic Movement*
GA 260   *The Christmas Conference*
GA 260a   *The Constitution of the School of Spiritual Science* or *The Life, Nature and
           Cultivation of Anthroposophy*
GA 262   *Correspondence and Documents*
GA 265   *Concerning the History and Content of the Higher Degrees of the Esoteric
           School, 1904–1914*
GA 266   *Esoteric Lessons 1904–1909*
GA 284/285 *Rosicrucianism Renewed*
GA 342   *Vorträge und Kurse über christlich-religiösen Wirken, I*
GA 346   *The Book of Revelation and the Work of the Priest*